*Richard C. Foltz*

# SPIRITUALITY
## IN THE LAND OF
# THE NOBLE

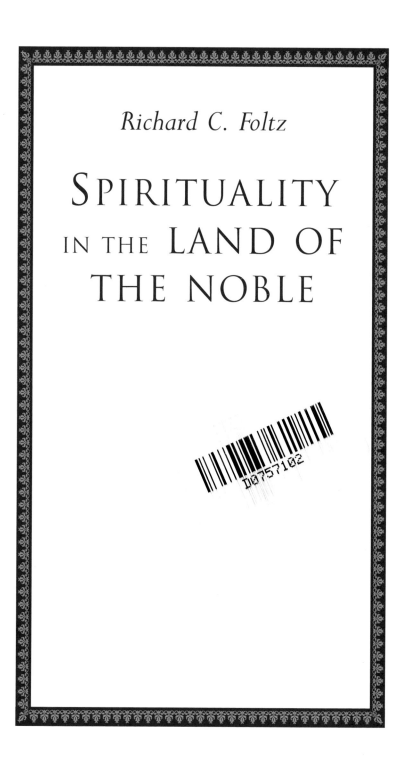

Richard C. Foltz

# SPIRITUALITY
## IN THE LAND OF
## THE NOBLE

*How Iran Shaped the World's Religions*

ONEWORLD
OXFORD

SPIRITUALITY IN THE LAND OF THE NOBLE

Oneworld Publications
(Sales and Editorial)
185 Banbury Road
Oxford OX2 7AR
England

www.oneworld-publications.com

ISBN 1–85168–333–X (hardback)
ISBN 1–85168–336–4 (paperback)

Typeset by Graphicraft Limited, Hong Kong
Cover design by Design Deluxe
Printed and bound in Singapore by Tien Wah Press Pte. Ltd

*For Désirée,*
*my love, my anchor, my friend*

# Contents

# *Preface*

When speaking of "cradles of religion" one most commonly thinks of the Near East and South Asia. The role of Iranians in generating and shaping the world's major religious traditions is not less than that of Semites or Indians, but it is less obvious. It is the aim of this book to bring that contribution into the foreground.

Of course Iran today is an overwhelmingly Muslim nation – about ninety-nine percent of the total population of over seventy million, nine-tenths of whom are Ithna 'Ashari Shi'is. But even in the world's first modern Islamic state there is far more religious diversity than meets the eye at first glance. The Iranian constitution reserves three seats in Parliament for representatives of the Christian minority, and one seat each for Jews and Zoroastrians. Only Baha'is – who, numbering as much as half a million or more in Iran, remain the country's largest non-Muslim minority – are denied official recognition and representation, while Iran's tiny community of ancient Gnostics, the Mandaeans, are hardly known at all.

Modern Iran's relative religious homogeneity notwithstanding, throughout the country's long history its peoples and cultures have played an unexcelled role in influencing, transforming, and propagating all the world's universal traditions. As I have described in another book, the merchants and missionaries who first brought Judaism, Buddhism, Christianity, Manichaeism, and Islam to China along the Silk Roads were predominantly Iranian. Along the way each of these traditions was dramatically infused with Iranian ideas and interpretations.

Apart from Zoroastrianism, Islam, and the Baha'i faith, the histories of other religions within Iran itself remain largely unexplored, although prior to the Arab conquest in the seventh century CE much of eastern Iran was Buddhist and much of the western regions Christian. Manichaeism, itself largely an Iranian product, was a major presence there for a number of centuries.

The history of Iranian Judaism, which begins with the fall of Israel to the Assyrians in 722 BCE and subsequent deportations of Israelites to Iranian territories, is one of the least-known aspects of the Jewish diaspora. The influence of Iranians and specifically Iranian notions in the foggy emergence of Mahayana Buddhism has only very recently begun to be seriously explored by scholars. And while Christianity's attempts to permeate the world's largest continent appeared by post-Mongol times to have been a spectacular failure (the Christianization of the Philippines and Korea being a more recent phenomenon), centuries earlier the balance between the eastern and western churches was far more even. For well over a millennium it was the Iranian variant of Christianity that Asians knew and perceived as normative, as the surprised (and dismayed) accounts of William of Rubruck and other early Catholic missionaries make clear.

The role of Iranians in shaping Islam and Muslim civilization – comparable perhaps to that of Hellenism in the formation of Christianity – is well understood by specialists but not so much by the general public. To this day most people continue to associate Islam with Arabs and the Near East, despite the fact that in Asia, where three-quarters of the world's Muslims actually live, Islam was received in most cases through a thickly Persian filter.

Finally there is the Baha'i faith, a distinctly modern religious tradition whose universalizing approach exceeds, and indeed attempts to subsume, all of its predecessors. Nothing evokes the Iranian origins of this now global religion more vividly than a visit to the beautiful Persian gardens surrounding Baha'i shrines of Acre and Haifa in Israel.

Why have the extraordinarily broad and profound influences of Iran on the world's religions gone so largely unnoticed for so long? Simple, authoritative answers are elusive, but a few tentative suggestions may be made. The comparative historical study of religions as an academic approach is fairly recent, as well as Western in origin and orientation, resulting in several fundamental biases. One such bias favors Classical Greek and Roman civilizations as superior models and primary sources of influence on later human societies. Another bias tends to define cultures in terms of key texts and the languages in which they were written, to the detriment of other sources whether textual or otherwise. Comparatively few such texts were originally composed in Persian or other Iranian languages.

The fact that historically, a preponderance of Iranian writers great and small have chosen to write in non-Iranian languages – whether Aramaic, Arabic, Sanskrit, Chinese, or English – has led to a situation where even in these enlightened times one still finds major Iranian figures like Avicenna, Ghazali, and Rhazes referred to as "Arab" writers. The thousand and one stories with which that brilliant Persian raconteuse, Shahrzad (Scheherezade), enthralled a mythical Persian king continue to be known by many as "The Arabian Nights." And how many in the West still find it hard to sort out (Persian) Iran and (Arab) Iraq?

Yet it takes but the faintest scratching to uncover the legions of important Iranians and Iranian ideas lurking beneath the literary veneers of world history. The task of this book, therefore, is a relatively easy one, consisting mainly of pointing out what ought to be clearly visible but has, like a finely crafted old table relegated to an over-stuffed storage room, for too long remained out of sight and under-appreciated.

I have transliterated Persian names and words according to current standard Persian pronunciation, except in cases where they apply to non-Iranian cultures or have familiar English forms (e.g., Muhammad, not Mohammad). Since so much has been written on Iranian Islam in comparison to other Iranian religions, the attempt to give them all equal time has been a challenge and has certainly resulted in some imbalances. Moreover, in a deliberately concise treatment many details and subtleties of argument must be omitted, some of them no doubt important ones. Of course, no one undertaking to write about so many different times and places can claim expertise in all of them. For these and any other shortcomings the author begs the reader's patience and indulgence.

I owe a great and enduring debt of thanks to my beautiful wife, Aphrodite Désirée Navab, scion of an old family of Esfahan, who for the past dozen years has kept my personal life firmly rooted in Iranian tradition. There is a Persian saying that you don't know where you are from until you get married, and though my study of Iran predates our partnership, our years together have provided perhaps the closest thing to a cultural anchor I have known in an otherwise often peripatetic life. To our daughter Shahrzad – a teller of tales even at the tender age of seven! – I hope that this book may one day help her more richly to imagine a land that she has seen and loved alas only briefly.

I would also like to thank the many Iranians I have known over the years, from my first Iranian friend, Saeed Akhtari, who initiated me into the Persian subculture of Salt Lake City, Utah, and my first teachers of Persian, Professors Mehdi Marashi and Leonardo Alishan who changed the course of my life, for better or for worse, from one of a perennial vagabond to that of a gainfully employed educator, to all of my many relatives by marriage in the United States, Iran, and elsewhere, and finally my Iranian-American students at the University of Florida, who so often excel their peers both in their respect for learning and their enthusiasm for it, at least when it comes to the culture of their parents. The example of all of these wonderful people has provided this erstwhile Calvinist with an endless lesson in proper hospitality, love for family, subtlety of expression, a broadened and creative approach to what constitutes truth, and the possibility of loving both the spirit and the world without contradiction – though I dare say I have often as not proved a disappointing student. I offer this book as a humble and entirely inadequate gesture of recognition and appreciation.

Earlier drafts of the typescript were read by Jason BeDuhn, Elton Daniel, Frederick Denny, Ruth Foltz, Richard Frye, Ahmad Khatoonabadi, Victor Mair, Moojan Momen, David Morgan, Aphrodite Désirée Navab, John Perry, Ehsan Yarshater, and an anonymous reader. Jacob Neusner offered useful comments on chapter three, Jorunn Jacobsen Buckley on the material pertaining to Mandaeans, Eden Naby on that relating to Assyrian Christians, and Safei Hamed on Persian gardens. I am deeply grateful for their comments and suggestions; any remaining errors are my own. My gratitude also goes to Sheldon Isenberg, Chair of the Department of Religion, and Neil Sullivan, Dean of the College of Arts and Sciences, at the University of Florida, for providing me with a paid research leave during the spring of 2003. Finally, I would like to thank the staff at Oneworld, and especially Novin Doostdar without whose encouragement and enthusiasm this book might never have been written.

Québec, QC
24 June 2003 (Fête nationale de St. Jean)
4 Tir 1382

# Historical Timeline

| | |
|---|---|
| ca. 4000 BCE | Proto-Indo-European speakers in Central Eurasia |
| ca. 2000–1000 BCE | Aryans migrate onto Iranian plateau |
| ca. 1750 BCE | Life of Abraham |
| ca. 1200–1000 BCE (?) | Life of Zoroaster (Zarathushtra) |
| 549–330 BCE | Achaemenid Empire |
| 539 BCE | Conquest of Babylonia by Cyrus the Great, liberation of Israelites and other subject peoples |
| ca. 500 BCE | Life of Gautama Buddha |
| 247 BCE–224 CE | Parthian Empire |
| 3 BCE–30 CE | Life of Jesus of Nazareth |
| ca. 100–300 CE | Mandaeans relocate from Palestine to southern Mesopotamia |
| 216–276 CE | Life of Mani |
| 224–651 CE | Sasanian Empire, codification of Zoroastrianism |
| 520s CE | Mazdakite movement |

| | |
|---|---|
| ca. 570–632 CE | Life of Muhammad |
| 641 CE | Arabs defeat Sasanian army at battle of Nehavand, begin conquest of Iran |
| 680 CE | Massacre of third Shi'ite Imam, Husayn, along with his followers, by forces of the Umayyad Caliph Yazid at Karbala in southern Iraq |
| 749–751 CE | Iran-based Abbasid revolution overthrows Umayyad dynasty |
| 816–837 CE | Rebellion of Babak |
| ca. 980–1010 CE | The *Book of Kings* (*Shah-nameh*) redacted into verse by Abo'l-Qasem Ferdowsi from various Iranian heroic epics |
| 1090–1256 CE | Assassins wage campaigns from base at Alamut castle |
| 1207–1273 CE | Life of mystic poet Jalal al-din Rumi |
| 1256–1336 CE | Mongol Il-Khan dynasty rules Iran |
| 1258 CE | Mongol conquest of Baghdad, end of Abbasid caliphate |
| 1370–1405 CE | Central Asian Turkic empire of Timur (Tamerlane) |
| 1501 CE | Foundation of Safavid Empire; formerly Sunni Iran becomes Twelver Shi'ite state |
| 1785–1925 CE | Qajar dynasty |
| 1819–1852 CE | Life of the Bab |
| 1817–1892 CE | Life of Baha'u'llah |
| 1925–1979 CE | Pahlavi dynasty |
| 1978–80 CE | Iranian revolution; Iran becomes Islamic Republic |
| 1997 CE | Mohammad Khatami becomes President of the Islamic Republic of Iran |

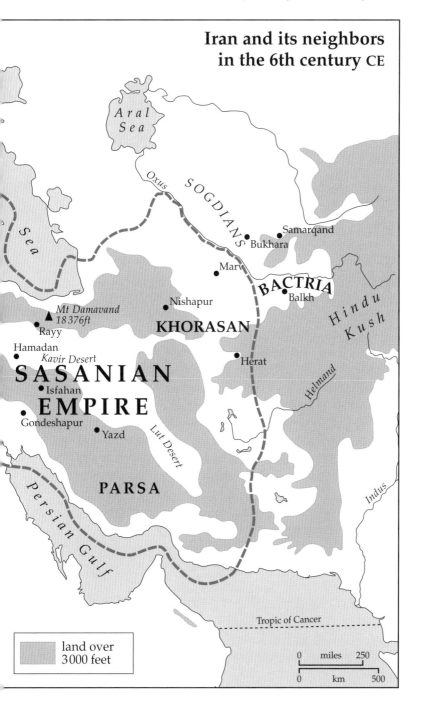

# Iran and its neighbors in the 6th century CE

Aral Sea

*Oxus*

SOGDIANS

Samarqand

Bukhara

Marv

BACTRIA

Balkh

*Sea*

*Mt Damavand 18 376ft*

Nishapur

KHORASAN

*Hindu Kush*

Rayy

Hamadan

*Kavir Desert*

Herat

*Helmand*

SASANIAN

Isfahan

EMPIRE

Gondeshapur

Yazd

*Lut Desert*

*Indus*

PARSA

*Persian Gulf*

Tropic of Cancer

land over
3000 feet

| 0 | miles | 250 |
|---|-------|-----|
| 0 | km | 500 |

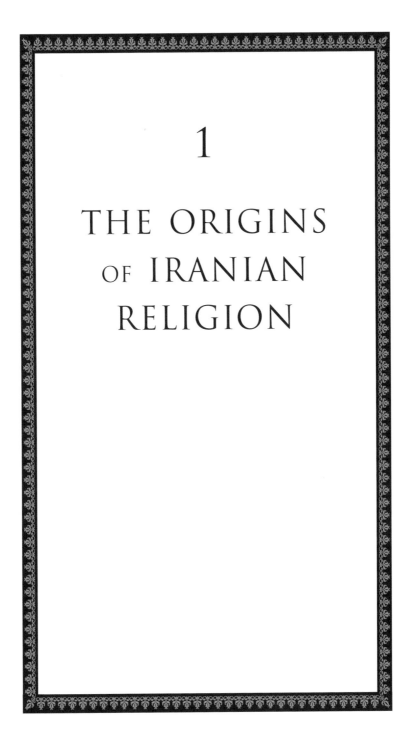

# 1

# THE ORIGINS OF IRANIAN RELIGION

## Iran and Iranianness

People generally feel proud of their own culture and nation, and rightly so, even if the reasons for that pride are not always strongly evident to outsiders. At any given point in history there are bound to be disparities between the relative assertiveness of some cultures compared to others, and the shadow of one culture may obscure the very different merits and contributions of others.

In the early twenty-first century, Iran (pronounced *ee-ron*, not, as is often heard, *eye-ran*) occupies something of a middle ground between dominant nations such as the United States and the many smaller countries which are continually confronted with the actions, policies and products of the former. While Iran is perhaps not one of the major players on the contemporary world scene, neither is it a country that can be affordably ignored.

Yet for much of human history over the past three millennia, Iran was as formidable a force as the U.S. is today, as Britain was in the nineteenth century, even as Rome was two thousand years ago. It was a culture, often *the* culture, to be reckoned with. Consequently Iranians, ever mindful that they are heirs to one of the world's oldest and most influential civilizations, often strike others as possessing a sense of cultural superiority that even the French would be hard put to match.

But how, exactly, should Iranian culture be defined? What constitutes entitlement to this rich legacy? Issues of nation, ethnicity and identity have never been more problematic or intensely debated as they are today, and I will make no attempt to settle the matter here. It is possible, however, to point out at least two features which have been strongly associated with Iranian identity throughout history. One is land – broadly speaking, the so-called Iranian plateau which occupies the nexus between the Caucasus mountains, the Mesopotamian plain, and the high mountain ranges of Central Asia. The other is language – broadly, again, the Iranian branch of the so-called Indo-European family of languages, but often more specifically the language known as Persian, which is the official language of the Islamic Republic of Iran as well as being one of the official languages of Afghanistan (where it is called Dari) and Tajikistan (where it is called Tojiki).[1] In past times it was also the administrative and literary language of such non-Iranian regions as India and Turkey. It is important to note that Iranian identity merely requires a strong *affinity* for the land and language, since many Iranians do not live in Iran, and many others even in Iran speak (or write) Persian only as a second language.

## Indo-Europeans and the search for origins

In Iran's case land and language came together during a period some three thousand years ago, following centuries of southerly migration by bands of Indo-European speakers[2] onto the Iranian plateau. Throughout this time they presumably came into contact with the region's existing inhabitants, with whom they mixed. This explains why it is a mistake to equate language with ethnicity, since when different human groups come into contact they typically blend their traditions over time but with some cultural artifacts – for example, the language of one group – eventually taking over at the expense of the other. Thus Etruscans, Aztecs, and others did not "die out" or become exterminated, so much as adopt the language (Latin, Spanish) and many of the customs and beliefs of their conquerors. The same is no doubt true for the pre-Indo-European inhabitants of Iran. Of course what is less apparent is the influences that went the other way, from conquered peoples to their conquerors, but in many cases these can be surmised, at least to some extent.

Since historically speaking this process of encounter and mutual influence ultimately takes the form of infinite regression, the same remarks could be made about the constitution of prehistoric Indo-European speakers of the steppes, whose racial homogeneity cannot be presumed. Their culture must already have been a composite of previous encounters between distinct groups of people. But beyond a certain point the horizon of history becomes an indecipherable blur.

So in attempting to reconstruct the cultural and belief system of the earliest Indo-Europeans, we must be content to abandon our quest for ultimate origins and focus our attention on the period about six thousand years ago, give or take a millennium or so, long before these peoples began their migration into what is now Iran. By applying the methodologies of historical linguistics to literary vestiges which survive in various Indo-European languages (such as Icelandic, German, Gaelic, Latin, Greek, Russian, Persian, Sanskrit, and many others including, of course, English), and combining this understanding with archeological evidence from areas where these languages came to be spoken, scholars have begun to form a picture of the culture of the prehistoric steppe peoples who spoke the ancestor language now referred to as "Proto-Indo-European," or PIE.

For example, common derivations of the name for the sky god worshiped by the PIEs, *Deiwo*,[3] can be found in many Indo-European languages: *Deus* in Latin, *Zeus* in Greek, and *Tiw* in Old English – Tuesday (Tiw's day) being originally devoted to him. The Iranian and Indian variants, *Dyaoš* and *Dyaus*, respectively, refer to a deity who had become remote and was no longer worshiped by the time the Avestan and Sanskrit texts were composed.

Efforts have also been made to reconstruct the PIE language itself, grammar as well as vocabulary, although, since the language was never written, such attempts are purely speculative. Among the thousands of Indo-European roots reconstructed by modern scholars, one finds the word *airyo*, meaning "noble." This ancient word appears to have represented a concept that PIE speakers considered to be of very great significance, even perhaps a central feature of their self-identification, since some of their descendants saw fit to use the word as a name for themselves (Aryan) and for the lands they came to occupy. Thus, the names of two modern countries, Ireland (Eire) and Iran, and one ancient one, Aryavarta (northwestern India in Vedic times), all mean "Land of the Noble."

The PIE-speaking peoples were pastoralists probably living in the area from what is now Ukraine to western Kazakhstan. Their existence was a precarious one even by prehistoric standards, since they occupied lands subject to an extreme continental climate of very cold winters and very hot summers, along with very little rainfall. They were a people living on the margins, both literally and metaphorically. To the great civilizations with which they were contemporary – those of Mesopotamia, Egypt, the Indus valley, and eventually China – they were entirely peripheral, though there must have been some occasional contact with Mesopotamia across the Caucasus mountains. And in terms of their subsistence lifestyle, the harsh ecology of their environment must have kept them more or less constantly on the edge of survival.

It may be assumed that the particular life circumstances of the PIE-speakers significantly influenced their culture and belief system. This hypothesis is consistent with much of what survives as distinctively Indo-European (or Aryan) elements in the worldviews of historical cultures, especially where these survivals seem more compatible with the realities of steppe pastoralism than, say, those of agrarian India or industrial Germany. Indeed, part of the enterprise of reconstructing this ancient culture, in the absence of any documents of its own, entails resituating what appear in their later forms to be anomalies – as in India with the Hindu *soma* ritual, which must be performed without access to *soma*, or the horse sacrifice, which was abandoned for scarcity of horses – into a putative "original" context.

If PIE-speakers had agriculture, it was minimal, constrained by the aridity and temperature extremes of their environment. They did keep domestic animals, especially cattle and sheep.[4] Indeed, wealth and social status were apparently measured mainly in terms of cattle ownership. (Even in historic Ireland, *bo airig*, "cattle-owning," was the Celtic term for a freeman.) The PIEs endowed the act of cattle raiding with a sacred importance, and raids were accompanied by a variety of rituals which included the drinking of intoxicating beverages. The oldest such drink was apparently mead; later they discovered wine and the mysterious *soma*.

Sharing their grassy landscape with grazing animals also provided another boon to the PIE peoples: at some point, perhaps four thousand years ago or even earlier, it occurred to someone to hitch up a horse and force it to pull a cart. To the PIEs would seem to go the credit for initiating the world's first great revolution in transportation technology, an innovation that would be central to their eventual success in spreading out and conquering much of the world. No wonder that the horse would become, alongside the bull, one of the most significant symbols in PIE religion, attested in copious examples of later Saka gold-work, the Greek myth of Apollo, the Vedic horse sacrifice, and elsewhere.

If the domestication of horses made PIEs the ancient world's most mobile people, their eventual mastery of metallurgy gave them the edge – a sword's edge, more often than not – over those with whom they came in contact, even when their opponents were "more culturally advanced" by almost any other measure. Again, ecological factors, so cruel in some respects, favored the PIEs in others. More so than any other human group of their time, PIEs were blessed by their proximity to horses, which could extend their range and speed beyond what any prior human group had known, and in the Ural and Altai mountains, to copper, tin, and eventually iron ore which could be smelted into durable weapons. A climate that kept their agricultural productivity to absolute subsistence levels ensured that a constant need to attack and steal from others would be a permanent feature of the PIE economy.

Here again, it comes as no surprise to find martial, and correspondingly, patriarchal, values as being highly esteemed in PIE society. The PIE class structure, echoes of which can be seen in the caste system of India, placed priests and chieftains at the top of the social pyramid, followed by a larger class of warriors, then herdsmen or other "producers."[5] When Aryan groups arrived in India, beginning some thirty-five centuries ago, they came to view the vast population of indigenous South Asians as a massive, fourth underclass.

In other words, PIE society was both highly authoritarian and distinctly stratified. The attribution of absolute authority to the leader survives in such notions as the English "divine right of kings" and the Iranian-Islamic concept of the king as "shadow of God on Earth." In PIE times the priests (think of the Druids of old Britain or the Brahmins of India) were the ones who knew the sacred formulas and rituals that could appease and maintain balance with the capricious supernatural forces such as storms, the alternately life-giving and scorching sun, and the various animal and other spirits whose goodwill or malice meant life or death for the community. Needless to say, in this warlike society martial deities such as the thunder god (the later Scandinavian Thor, Slavic Perun) received special attention and tribute.

As mentioned above, the major sources for reconstructing PIE culture are archeological evidence and later texts. Artifacts from the ground are hard to interpret in the absence of supplementary data (imagine trying to reconstruct the beliefs and practices of Christianity on the basis of nothing more than a dug-up old crucifix and a chalice), but extrapolation from later written sources can help one at least to make thoughtful guesses.

One technique is to comb through available literature, such as myths, in various Indo-European languages, and look for apparent commonalities. After centuries of oral transmission in diverse locales one would hardly expect the stories to remain the same, but if similarities exist they may indicate a common origin. If this process of collation and comparison turns up identifiable characters, plots and themes in stories from ancient Greece and India, medieval Germany and Iceland, and perhaps elsewhere, as it turns out is often the case, then the common elements may have been present as far back as the period of the original PIE language, and may even be older than that. Obviously any differences between the stories can be attributed to later variations in storytelling to suit local contexts.

Once a core "original" version of a myth or an idea is distilled out in this way, it can be applied to the interpretation of archeological data. Thus, if a small four-thousand-year-old winged horse figure carved from stone turns up in a dig in Central Asia, its original use and significance may be assessed in terms of reconstructed proto-myths about winged horses. Frustratingly, we can never know for sure if the conclusions we are drawing are accurate, and the best guesses of the best scholars are forever being questioned and reevaluated.

The oldest extant Indo-European literary source is the Rig Veda, considered by Hindus to be a sacred text. Its present form dates probably to around the eighth century BCE ("Before the Common Era"),[6] but its content is much older. In fact, the world it evokes resembles not the steamy plains of northwest India, but rather the dry steppes of western

Eurasia whence the Indo-Aryans came. Because it recalls the original PIE homeland, and especially because it shows so many similarities with the oldest Iranian text, the Avesta, the Rig Veda can shed light on the origins of Iranian religion as much as it can for Hinduism – perhaps even more so, since Hinduism retains much that presumably predates the Aryan arrival.[7] The harsh, remote environment depicted in the Rig Veda is the one from which the Aryans of Iran and India both came.

The Vedas (the term is derived from the idea of knowledge, cognate with the English "wisdom" and "wit") are often described as "hymns," though to contemporary ears this might give a misleading impression. They are formulaic incantations, known only to the privileged priestly class and memorized in order to be performed under specific circumstances and in a strictly defined way. Even by the time the first Brahmin priests transcribed them twenty-seven centuries ago these verses were no longer completely understood, but that surely bothers us more than it would have concerned them. As with any magical undertaking, the important thing was to "do it exactly right," not necessarily to comprehend what was being done as long as the desired result was obtained.

The excerpt from the Rig Veda which follows is dedicated to Soma, which is at once a substance and a deity. The substance itself, which was ritually processed into a drink, has been the subject of much speculation, since it has apparently not been available as such since PIE times. What is clear is that it was a powerful hallucinogen. Some scholars have guessed a beverage concocted from hallucinogenic mushrooms, others from a plant, such as ephedra. (Considerable scientific effort has been expended trying to replicate this marvelous drug!) Presumably we are dealing with a source organism endemic to western Eurasia, since in ancient India and Iran alike priests were unable to make it and had to use innocuous substitutes.

It may be helpful to prepare for reading the following example by taking a moment to close one's eyes and mentally picture oneself as a part of the ancient steppe world. Sitting around a campfire with family and friends beneath a crisp Montana sky might inspire the appropriate sort of image. Earth and the heavens recede in all directions, meeting each other beyond the horizon. The sun sets, cows low and horses whinny nearby. Add the tension of some imminent threat – a looming storm, a band of strangers in the distance – and look to those among you most gifted with insight to guide the course your group will take. They know the techniques for transcending mundane reality, for bridging the seen and the unseen. Soma is one such technique.

Slowly, carefully, methodically, your priests bring out the Soma bowl and implements. Using means known only to themselves, they prepare the sacred nectar by which they will collapse the boundaries between heaven and earth, human and divine. They finish their preparations and drink the Soma.

> This, yes this is my thought: I will win a cow and a horse. Have I not drunk Soma?
>
> Like impetuous winds, the drinks have lifted me up. Have I not drunk Soma?
>
> The drinks have lifted me up, like swift horses bolting with a chariot. Have I not drunk Soma?
>
> The prayer has come to me as a lowing cow comes to her beloved son. Have I not drunk Soma?
>
> I turn the prayer around in my heart, as a wheelwright turns a chariot seat. Have I not drunk Soma?
>
> The five tribes are no more to me than a mote in the eye. Have I not drunk Soma?
>
> The two world halves cannot be set against a single wing of mine. Have I not drunk Soma?
>
> In my vastness, I surpassed the sky and this vast earth. Have I not drunk Soma?
>
> Yes! I will place the earth here, or perhaps there. Have I not drunk Soma?
>
> I will thrash the earth soundly, here, or perhaps there. Have I not drunk Soma?
>
> One of my wings is in the sky; I have trailed the other below. Have I not drunk Soma?
>
> I am huge, huge! flying to the cloud. Have I not drunk Soma?
>
> I am going to a well-stocked house, carrying the oblation to the gods. Have I not drunk Soma?[8]

One student who read this passage explained to my class that the popular party drug Ecstasy provides much the sensation described in this ancient text. Interestingly, a pharmacy student in the same class added that the chemical properties of Ecstasy are similar to those in ephedrine – ephedra, remember, being one of the candidates for the original Soma plant. In any event it is easy to see why Indian and Iranian priests bemoaned the fact that the substance could no longer be produced in their adopted lands.

The Soma drinker not only collapses the boundaries between heaven and earth (i.e., earth and sky, the "two worlds"), he effaces any distinction between himself and the divine. The Soma, being at once substance and divinity, courses through his veins, metabolizes within him. Space and time no longer confine him; he can fly anywhere, see anything. The resonance of this tradition spans the human experience, since it is surely very old and because the shamanic experience of "flying," breaking all barriers of time and space, is so widespread in human cultures.[9]

## Features of old Iranian religion

Taking advantage of their unique, horse-assisted mobility, and perhaps spurred on by unfavorable climatic events, the ancient Proto-Indo-European-speaking tribes split up over time as smaller groups branched off and went their separate ways. Among the first to strike off on their own must have been the ancestors of the Celts, who went west, and the Tokharians (partial ancestors of the modern Uighurs in western China), who went east, since their descendant languages differ most dramatically from the other Indo-European tongues.

A little less than four thousand years ago certain Indo-European bands, who can be collectively referred to as Indo-Iranians, began moving southwards along the eastern side of the Caspian Sea.[10] Eventually they too split up, with some continuing southeastwards across what is now Afghanistan and into the Indian subcontinent, and others, the ancestors of modern Iranians, continuing south onto the Iranian plateau. A few early adventurers made their way to Mesopotamia and attained positions within the ruling class there.

The oldest literary vestiges of the Indo-Aryans and their ancient Iranian cousins, namely the Rig Veda and the Avesta, are similar enough in both language and content that, when compared with each other and with later Hindu and Zoroastrian writings, they suggest a fairly detailed picture of what the Indo-Iranians did and believed. Again, archeological finds tend to be weighed against what is understood from these texts through a process of what we might call "critical backward projection."

## CREATION AND THE NATURE OF THE UNIVERSE

Ancient Iranians believed that the universe was created in seven stages – the number "seven" having a lasting mystical significance and widespread influence in later cultures. First was created the sky, then water, earth, plants, animals, humans, and finally, fire. Exactly what force or forces they believed set the process of creation in motion is not clear (for many of the world's ancient peoples, the problem of original agency is of far less concern than it is in later philosophical traditions). Originally the universe was static; then the first plant, the first animal (a bull), and the first human (Yima, or Jamshid; Sanskrit Yama), were all sacrificed and their seeds dispersed, setting the cycle of death and rebirth in motion.

The sky was imagined as a vast sphere encompassing the earth, but viewed from human perspective as an inverted bowl of brilliant stone. Water was thought to flow beneath the earth, which floated upon it like a plate. The tallest mountain, Haraberezaiti (Harburz, Hara), reached so high that it pierced heaven, and the sun, moon, and stars all revolved around it. A distant memory of this belief is echoed in the name of Iran's northern mountain range, the Alborz, which includes the country's highest peak, Mount Damavand.

Indo-Iranians divided the world into seven climes,[11] of which they believed theirs, Khvaniratha, to be the largest, central, and most pleasant. The various rivers, mountains, and other natural features which appear in the myths are difficult to associate with actual places, since the ancient Iranians were mobile and probably shifted their identifications in keeping with their changing locales. Migrants typically give old names to new places, as a glance at any map of the USA will amply illustrate. Ancient Iranians called their immediate territory Airyana Vaejah – meaning, like the Vedic Aryavarta, "Land of the Noble" – but this would have referred to different actual locations at different periods in their prehistory.

## SUPERNATURAL BEINGS

Like most ancient (and some modern) peoples, the Indo-Iranians saw an association between supernatural beings – which they called *mainyu*s (Vedic *manyu*) – and natural phenomena. Meteorological forces and animate and inanimate objects were identified each with their own spirit dimension, as were abstract notions like fate and moral qualities. Nature deities included the sun, the moon, the sky, fire, water, and wind, as well as specific items like the soma plant mentioned above. The most important cosmological principle was the concept of a universal order of Truth – the Sanskrit word *rta*, the Old Persian *arta*, and the Avestan *asha* all being cognate with English "right." Different deities were seen each as playing their own role in upholding this cosmic order. An opposing principle, *drug*, accounted for disorder and calamity. Iranians would eventually come to see the world in terms of an ongoing struggle between these two opposing forces.

Another abstract idea which would become a central feature in the Iranian worldview was that of heavenly blessing, called *khvarna* (*farr*, in modern Persian). Those thus favored by the gods would enjoy success and prosperity, while its withdrawal led to all manner of misfortune and disaster. Heroes, kings, and prophets owe their glory to this divine investiture, which is symbolized in later Persian painting as golden flames leaping up from around the figure's head. (In later times even the Buddha and the prophet Muhammad are portrayed in this way.)

Among the other divine beings, one major class was a group of benevolent deities known in India as *asura*s and in Iran as *ahura*s. (The word, which means "lord," may first have been applied to tribal elders and only later to deities.) Another grouping, more morally ambiguous, was called *deva*s in India and *daeva*s in Iran. The *ahura*s employed magical powers to intervene in world events, while the *daeva*s, characterized mainly by their strength, were particularly favored by warriors. According to Georges Dumézil, the Proto-Indo-Europeans classified their deities into three broad groupings which mirrored the tripartite structure of their own society comprising priests/rulers, warriors, and commoners. Reflections of this paradigm can be found in the mythologies of all Indo-European peoples, Indo-Iranians included. Thus the gods Mitra and Varuna are associated with the priestly group, Indra with the warriors, and fertility deities with the more numerous "producers."[12]

Certainly one of the oldest forms of human religiosity is the worship of ancestors and departed heroes, an impulse which survived among the Indo-Iranians. *Fravashi*s, as ancestor spirits were known to the ancient Iranians, could help and protect their living relatives, providing of course that they were properly remembered and propitiated. The afterlife was originally thought of as a dreary existence in a dark underworld, although passages in the Rig Veda together with archeological evidence indicate an emerging belief in bodily resurrection by around thirty-five hundred years ago.

RITES AND PRACTICES

Based mainly on archeological evidence dating as far back as seven thousand years, scholars have supposed that the oldest Indo-European ritual traditions included the veneration of sky and earth deities, ancestor worship, and cults of fire and water. Traces of all of these are detectable in the various later Indo-European cultures. Among the oldest rituals, attested by excavated objects and through surviving rituals in later cultures, appear to have been the regular pouring of libation offerings to bodies of water and the burning of offerings such as animal fat to the hearth fire, which was kept going (in the form of embers) even when traveling. Ritual vessels were "purified" using cow urine, rich in ammonia. In the Indo-Iranian society of the third millennium BCE there were apparently several basic categories of priests. The most important were the libation-pourers, called *zaotar*s. (The prophet Zoroaster was a member of this group.) Another type of priest was the *atharvan*, charged with keeping the sacred fire. A third group, the *kavi*s, had the knowledge of magic and immortality. Finally there were the *usig*s, who accompanied the warriors on cattle raids.

Ancient Indo-European societies did not have governments or police forces to maintain order. Social cohesion and stability were ensured through mutually agreed-upon codes and conventions. Preliterate peoples tend to place a great importance on orality, and Indo-Iranians in particular developed a strong affinity for spoken pacts, which essentially served as the society's legal system. Pacts had more than a merely temporal legal importance, however, since their proper observance was the means for upholding the cosmic order (*arta/asha*) while failure to do so would lead to chaos (*drug*).

One type of pact performed by the PIEs was the *mithra*, a covenant between two parties, the other being a *varuna* or individual oath. (Among the Iranians the *varuna* became subsumed by other deities.) In keeping with their belief about the supernatural inhering in abstract notions as well as in material things, Indo-Iranians personified the spiritual qualities (*mainyu*s) of these verbal pacts as powerful and important deities. The veracity of one's oral proclamations could be put to the test, through fire ordeal in the case of *mithra*s and water in the case of *varuna*s, which may explain why Mithra and Varuna, who were responsible for sparing the truthful and punishing the unworthy, became such important gods.

Our most abundant evidence for the particular behaviors of Indo-Iranians pertains mainly to the priestly class, since priests were the ones who memorized and passed on to future generations the sacred formulas (*manthra*s; Sanskrit *mantra*) which eventually came to be written down in religious texts like the Rig Veda and the Avesta. Thus, much of the written material available to us is associated with forms of sacrifice, called *yajna* in the former text and *yasna* in the latter.

The word "sacrifice" should be understood here not to emphasize so much the dimension of "giving up something valued," but more the original literal sense of "making [something] sacred." In general the purpose of this is to create a situation of sharing – a communion – between humans and the divine. Often this takes the form of a shared meal, which is why the food offering must be "made sacred" (i.e., "sacrificed") so that it is acceptable to the divine co-participant. Usually the bulk of the ritual consists of performing the appropriate preparations, incantations, and the like for bringing about the required transformation of the object to be sacrificed.

The most basic form of sacrifice entails a ritual reenactment of some pivotal primordial event, collapsing time as it were to bring the present together with the distant past (what Mircea Eliade calls *in illo tempore*, "in *that* time"). Thus to some extent at least, the enduring popularity of bull sacrifice, the crushing and consuming of soma, and perhaps occasionally human sacrifice, would seem to reenact aspects of the original creation myth. Sacrificial instructions from an ancient Indian text, the *Aitareya Brahmana*, show how the dismemberment of the victim was intended to nourish and regenerate all the vital elements of the living world:

Lay his feet down to the north. Cause his eye to go to the sun. Send forth his breath to the wind, his life-force to the atmosphere, his ears to the cardinal points, his flesh to the earth. Thus, the priest places the victim in these worlds.[13]

Before performing this sacrifice the Indo-Iranians would lay out a bed of sacred grass (Sanskrit *barhis*, Avestan *baresman*) as a "throne" for the deity being invited; the sacrificial victim would then be laid out upon it. In later Iranian religion the sacred grass became the bundle of "twigs" (*barsom* – now wires) used by Zoroastrian priests.

Many different types of sacrifices are described in the ancient texts, however. As might be expected in a military society, much of the Rig Veda involves sacrifices to the war god, Indra, whose martial qualities are lauded in a way that suggest a sort of warrior ideal or role model. Sacrifices to Soma are also very prominent. The latter substance/deity figures in the Avesta as well, under the variant *haoma*, although somewhat more ambivalently as we shall see in the following chapter.

Other rituals were connected with lesser deities, and with life-cycle events such as birth, puberty, marriage, and death. For non-priests, apparently the primary religious duties were to pray to the gods three times a day (at sunrise, midday, and sunset), to keep their hearth fires burning and maintain the purity of their vital water sources, and finally, materially to support their priests, who performed the ritual sacrifices (*yasna*) on behalf of the entire community.

Unfortunately the extent of our knowledge – or more accurately, our best guesses – about the nature and details of Indo-Iranian religious beliefs and practices does not extend very far beyond what has been briefly sketched out here. We know much more about those which existed later in India, by which time the Aryans had mingled their culture with that of the original South Asians, and in the Iranian world following the reforms of the prophet Zarathushtra (Zoroaster). It is to the contributions of this remarkable figure that we know turn.

# 2

# ZOROASTRIANISM

Among the founders of the world's major religious faiths, none is more shrouded in mystery than Zoroaster. Basic questions such as where and when he lived remain unresolved. Although the dates, places, and personal biographies associated with Abraham, Moses, the Buddha, Jesus, and Muhammad are still open to varying degrees of discussion, the range of uncertainty nowhere approaches that facing students of Zoroastrianism.

For example, it has been proposed that Zoroaster lived as early as the time of Abraham (eighteenth century BCE), or as late as the Buddha (sixth to fifth centuries BCE). Some ancient Greek sources even place him as far back as six thousand years before their own time! It has been argued that he lived in what is now Kazakhstan, beyond the northeastern fringe of the Iranian world, while others place him as far west as Azerbaijan. Much of the confusion arises from the fact that once a kind of Zoroastrianism had spread throughout the Iranian world, priests in various parts of Iran concocted legends (or distorted existing ones) connecting the prophet with their own regions. Some scholars, notably Jean Kellens, have suggested that Zoroaster is a fictional character who never existed at all.

The heroic epic tradition, which arose as a sort of semi-mythological genealogy for local rulers in eastern Iran, wove in various strands of Zoroaster stories taken from diverse traditions. (This process culminated in the tenth century with the poet Abo'l-Qasem Ferdowsi's version of the *Shah-nameh* or "Book of Kings," often referred to as the Persian national epic.) Priests who compiled or composed the Zoroastrian religious books during the Sasanian period (224–651 CE) selectively redacted their version of Iranian pre-history from the vast body of existing oral tradition (and possibly some lost texts) in accordance with their own particular agendas.

Most of what is reliably known about Zoroaster derives from philological analysis of the Zoroastrian holy book, the Avesta. But while certain passages of this scripture are surely very archaic, the version available to us dates only as far back as the early Christian era, many centuries after the prophet himself must have lived. Even more perplexing is the fact that the written sources of the great Achaemenid Persian Empire (549–330 BCE) fail to mention him at all, whereas a number of Greek sources do.

For these and other reasons it is probably preferable to reserve the term "Zoroastrianism" for the religion adopted and codified by the Sasanian Iranian state from the third century CE onward (even though the Sasanians never used the term themselves, calling it simply *veh-din*, "the Good Religion"). Iranian religiosity prior to that time must have differed considerably from one locality to another, with each local culture playing its own variations upon ancient Iranian themes and occasionally drawing in non-Iranian influences from neighboring peoples.

Certain developing notions, like the rising preeminence of the *ahura* of wisdom, Mazda, who was associated with the sun, and an increasingly sophisticated eschatology and soteriology, among other things, became widely present among dispersed Iranian societies throughout the first millennium BCE. Other beliefs and practices, such as particular hero cults, were more strictly local in nature, the hero-cult of Siyavash in Bukhara being one example. The codification and state-enforced adoption of a Zoroastrian faith based on the Avesta in Sasanian times would appear to be a case of one form of Iranian devotion rising suddenly to prominence, mainly for political reasons, and using its powerful resources to push competing versions of Iranian religion into the margins. Since many Iranian groups, including the imperial Achaemenids but also the nomadic Sakas (Scythians), seem to have worshipped Ahura Mazda but not necessarily known of Zoroaster, some scholars have proposed referring to pre-Sasanian Iranian religion as "Mazdaism."

## In search of Zoroaster

The oldest evidence for Zoroaster is found in the portions of the Avesta known as the Gathas – literally, "poems" or "verses" – which are believed to be the preserved words of Zoroaster himself. The language of these verses is archaic in the extreme, and very close to that of the Rig Veda. Like most ancient works of literature, including the epics of Homer and the Hebrew Bible, both of these texts were transmitted orally from one generation to the next over the course of many centuries before eventually being written down.

The language of sacred oral literature tends to change far more slowly than regular spoken dialects, if at all, and even in its original context may have represented a special, lofty form of speech rather than an idiom people ordinarily spoke. In the case of the Gathas, the absence of any other examples of the language in which they are preserved makes for very difficult comprehension even after a lifetime of study. So as a source for information about the life and times of Zoroaster, the Gathas leave much that is unclear or untold. Nevertheless, they provide a kind of rough portrait that can be compared with other evidence such as the rest of the Avesta, Greek sources, and the Zoroastrian books of Sasanian times.

The name Zarathushtra – Zoroaster being derived from the form used by the ancient Greeks – means something like "camel-manager," which gives some clue about the man and the kind of society he lived in. The Gathas depict a pastoral but settled form of society and a geography compatible with the steppes of Inner Asia. The languages of the Avesta, both that of the Gatha verses and of the remainder, called the "Younger Avesta," are very closely related Iranian dialects, distinct from those of the Median, Achaemenid, and Parthian records of western Iran.

The Younger Avesta contains a number of identifiable place names which have been located within the general area of eastern Iran, but the Gathas seem to be set further north. This may be due to the southward movement of the Indo-Iranians throughout the second millennium BCE. On the other hand, the Gathan and Younger Avestan languages may be more contemporaneous dialects from these adjacent regions, and the "Younger Avesta" might not in fact be "younger" as many scholars have assumed.

On the basis of linguistic evidence for the most part, Mary Boyce posits a dating for Zoroaster of around 1200 BCE. Gherardo Gnoli, meanwhile, having reviewed Boyce's and other arguments, concludes that the Zoroastrians' own traditional reference point situating him "258 years prior to Alexander" is basically valid. Gnoli argues for a set of dates earlier posited by Boyce's teacher, W. B. Henning, placing Zoroaster's lifetime from 618–541 BCE. Gnoli's recent conclusions have left many scholars unconvinced, however.

At present, it must be conceded that questions about Zoroaster's time and homeland have still not been definitively resolved. Nor is there any evidence that can suggest when and by what means Zoroaster's teaching was transmitted from the eastern Iranian world to the western regions which were home to the great Iranian empires; all we can say with certainty is that, somehow, sometime, it was.

Zoroaster was a member of the priestly class, living at a time when his society was undergoing internal tension and change. Apparently certain elements in Aryan society were inclining more towards the raiding aspect of their mixed pastoral economy, living by theft in preference to pasturing. (This may have been fostered by the development of the war chariot and bronze weapons; in Inner Asia both of these technologies arose during the first part of the second millennium BCE.) The resulting violence and chaos would have seemed to some, Zoroaster included, as an indication that *asha* (order) was giving way to *drug* (chaos). Yet in the minds of others, no doubt, bullying inferiors was the right way to go. In the Rig Veda, for example, brave Aryan warriors, supported by Indra, take great pride in their ability to steal from the hapless natives of South Asia, to whom they refer by the derisive term *dasa*s.

## Zoroaster's reform

One may suppose that by Zoroaster's time the rowdier of his fellow Aryans had turned the ancient rituals into little more than raucous orgies. It is not hard to imagine the moral indignation and outrage of a conscientious priest surrounded by soma-intoxicated partiers reveling in the bloodbath of a cow sacrifice. Yasna 29 in the Avesta richly evokes a situation where the champions of injustice had thrown the cosmic balance into a hopeless state of disorder, causing unwarranted suffering to man and beast alike:

The Soul of the Cow lamented to you: For whom have you determined me? Who fashioned me? Wrath and Violence, Harm, Daring, and Brutality [each] have bound me! I have no other pastor than you – so appear to me with good husbandry!

Then the Fashioner of the Cow asked Asha: Hast thou a *ratu* (priest) for the Cow such that you are able to give him, together with a herdsman, zeal for fostering the Cow? Whom do you want as a lord for her, who, hostile toward Liars, may repel Wrath? . . .

Mazda is most mindful of the declarations (*varuna*s) which have been made previously by *daeva*s and men and those which shall be made afterward, [for] he is the decisive Lord. Thus may it be for us as he may will!

Thus we are both calling out to the Lord with outstretched hands, my [soul] and the Soul of the pregnant Cow, in order that we may address Mazda with questions. [For as matters now stand] there is no possibility of continuing life for the righteously living husbandman [residing] among Liars.

Then Ahura Mazda, knowing, spoke [these] words through his life-breath: Not one [of us] has found an *ahu* (powerful man), not even a *ratu* in accordance with Truth. So, indeed, the Artificer fashioned thee for the husbandman and the herdsman.

Ahura Mazda, in agreement with Asha, fashioned the *manthra* of [something from] butter and [also] milk for the Cow, he [who] through [his] commandment is beneficial for those who are undernourished. Whom dost thou have [for us] through Good Mind (Vohu Mana), who will give us two to men?

Here I have found this one who alone listens to our commandments, Zarathushtra the Spitamid. He wants, O Mazda, to recite hymns of praise for us and Asha, if I should bestow on him sweetness of speech.

The Soul of the Cow lamented: Must I suffer a powerless caretaker – the speech of a man without strength – whom I wish to be a powerful ruler? When ever shall he come to exist who can give him a helping hand?

O Lord, may you [*ahura*s] give power and dominion (*khshathra*) to them, that [dominion] through Vohu Mana by which he might grant good living and peace. I, in any case, consider Thee, O Mazda, to be the original possessor of this.

Where are Asha and Vohu Mana and Khshathra? Now you should accept me, through Asha, O Mazda, for [giving] instruction to the great community. O Lord, [come] now to us [here] below on account of our liberality to such as you.[1]

In terms of the ancient Iranian religion outlined in the Introduction, one can detect much in this passage that is revolutionary. Most significant is that the *ahura* of Wisdom, Ahura Mazda, is elevated here above all other deities. He is "the decisive Lord," whose judgments are binding upon gods and humans alike. *Daeva*s and men are to be mindful that he (not, for example, Mitra or Varuna) is the force which will hold them accountable for their oaths and covenants. It is through his commandment that the undernourished receive their sustenance. He is "the original possessor" of "power and dominion (*khshathra*)," which are to be used not for oppression but for the maintenance of "good living and peace." All other divine forces and qualities, including "Good Mind" and even Truth itself, are only instruments of his will.

Whereas in prior Iranian cosmology creative agency was dispersed or unattributed, this role is said now to belong to Ahura Mazda. The all-powerful Creator, he is the proper focus of devotion and supplication. If monotheism ranks as one of the major innovations in the history of religious thought, then Israelites and Iranians must share the credit (or blame) for its conceptualization three thousand or more years ago.

The passage above is also remarkable in that it establishes a unique role for a single individual, Zoroaster. In a world given over to violent champions of the Lie, he is the only one who listens to Ahura Mazda's commandments; it is he who has been appointed to "give instruction to the great community," even though his power is that of words alone, since he is "a powerless caretaker . . . a man without strength." There is also a foreshadowing here of Zoroaster's fate, that of a prophet ignored in his own country, since the one "who can give him a helping hand" will be the distant chieftain Vishtaspa, and not one of Zoroaster's own tribe.

In perceiving Ahura Mazda as the Creator force, Zoroaster also attributed a purposefulness to Creation which was apparently not present in earlier Iranian thought. Zoroaster's ethics emphasized human choice: both good and bad existed in the world (conceptualized as *asha* and *drug*), and it was up to the individual to take a position and actively embrace one or the other. The world then was properly understood as a stage on which this human drama would be played out.

This thinking in turn implied a much stronger eschatology than in the existing worldview inherited from the Proto-Indo-Europeans. While the usual conception of time in ancient human societies was cyclical, Zoroaster saw it as a linear progression heading towards a great culminating event. He understood the universe as a battleground for an ongoing struggle between the forces of good and evil, a struggle in which each individual human being must take a side. The final resolution would come at the end of time in a great battle, called Frashokereti (literally, the "making glorious"), in which good would ultimately prevail.

Against this backdrop of cosmic conflict Zoroaster seems to have refined his society's conception of supernatural beings in terms of which side they were on. The *daeva*s, popular among the warrior class, came to be seen as being on the side of evil, giving rise to the notion of demons. (The Iranian word *daeva* is the ultimate source of the English word "devil.") Beneficent spirits, which Zoroaster called *yazata*s, literally "beings worthy of worship," became the model for what later societies would identify as angels. Zoroaster seems to have been the first of the world's major religious thinkers to posit a self-existent evil deity, elevating Aeshma, the *mainyu* of fury, as a polar opposite to Ahura Mazda. Called Angra Mainyu – "the hostile spirit" – in the Younger Avesta, and Ahriman in later sources, this evil god is the basis for the figure Semitic peoples would later call Satan.

Another significant innovation that is apparent in Zoroaster's thought is an elaboration on the ultimate fate of individuals as a result of the choices they make during their lives. Zoroaster seems to have been the first to articulate fully the notion of a posthumous judgment, where each person's good deeds would be weighed against their evil ones, following which the good people (*ashavan*) would ascend to the heavenly realm presided over by Ahura Mazda while the evildoers (*drugvant*) would descend to a hell of suffering ruled by Angra Mainyu. This judgment occurred at Mount Hara on the fourth day after death; the deceased would then cross a bridge, called Chinvat. For the *ashavan*, the bridge would grow wide and easy to cross, whereas for the *drugvant* it would become as narrow as a blade. The good would be met along the way by a beautiful female spirit, Daena, a reflection of their own inner goodness, who would accompany them to heaven. (Daena, originally a personification of individual character, much later evolves into the simple abstract notion of religion itself, *din*.) Wrongdoers, on the other hand, would find a horrible, smelly hag, in whose embrace they would plunge over the edge into the gaping mouth of hell.

The belief in an ultimate bodily resurrection also can be dated to Zoroaster. This would occur after the final defeat of the forces of evil by those of good at the end of time. All beings, good and bad, will have to pass through a river of fire; the good will be saved by the Yazatas, while the bad will be utterly destroyed, and thus will evil be banished from the world once and for all. The earth will blossom and the good will live forever in Mazda's divine kingdom. It is not clear whether the belief in an eschatological savior figure, who is known in Zoroastrian texts as the Saoshyant, dates from Zoroaster's time or later. Eventually the belief emerged that the Saoshyant would be born of Zoroaster's own seed, miraculously preserved in a lake in which a future virgin would bathe and become impregnated.

The Gathas make it clear that Zoroaster was rejected by his own community. He is said to have found a home among another group of Iranians some distance away, where he converted a chieftain by the name of Vishtaspa after first winning over the ruler's wife to his new teaching. (It is an interesting pattern in the spread of religions that religious teachers often have their greatest successes with royal womenfolk. Perhaps aristocratic women had more time on their hands to devote to their intellectual and spiritual curiosity? It is impossible to say.)

With Vishtaspa's support and patronage Zoroaster spent the rest of his reportedly long life training followers in "the Mazda-worshipping religion" and sent missionaries to preach his message far and wide. Presumably this activity was carried out mainly among neighboring Iranian groups, although one sees later echoes of Zoroastrian concepts among non-Iranians as far afield as Asia Minor and even China.

Apparently Zoroaster's ideas were often seen as a threat, since there are hints in the Avesta and elsewhere to his missionaries being persecuted and even killed. The same sources state that such persecutions only strengthened the resolve of Zoroaster's followers, and that their steadfast example inspired many others to join the faith. Though there may be an element of propaganda in this, the fact that eventually most Iranian tribes came to adopt at least some forms of Zoroaster's teaching shows that his ideas were ultimately spread successfully.

It should be noted that in the context of the ancient world the very notion of religious proselytizing was uncommon or even absent altogether, and to most people would probably have seemed highly unnatural. What we think of today as "religion" was not perceived as something apart from the general culture of a community. People likely would not have thought in terms of one religion (or culture) being "truer" or less so than another, but simply different, and one's adherence would be unquestioningly to the norms of one's own group. What one "believed" was of far less importance than what one did. Against this backdrop, Zoroaster's emphasis on correct belief and on personal choice and responsibility must have been quite revolutionary.

## *Zoroastrian practice*

The main ritual practice Zoroaster enjoined of his followers was to pray five times a day. To the traditional three daily devotions of the Aryans he added prayers at dawn and at midnight. The devotee of Ahura Mazda was always to pray standing in the presence of fire, either the sun or the sacred hearth. The ancient Aryan sacred cord, which boys received at puberty (a tradition found also in the Vedas), was to be tied and untied around the waist at every prayer. Zoroaster apparently extended this formerly male-only custom to women as well.

Within each Zoroastrian household one member was responsible for maintaining the sacred fire, which must never be allowed to go out. This became the most visible identification of Zoroastrians to outside observers such as the ancient Greeks. After the Arab conquests of the seventh century CE, Muslim writers derisively – and inaccurately – referred to Zoroastrians as "fire worshippers."

Zoroastrians were to show reverence and gratitude to all of natural creation, and strive always to maintain its purity, since everything in nature is indwelt with its own *mainyu*. Water sources especially were to be scrupulously protected, as was the sanctity of the soil. Since dead bodies were seen as polluting, Zoroastrians eventually abandoned the practice of burial in favor of exposure in "towers of silence," leaving corpses to be picked clean by vultures and the bones bleached pure by the sun.

For priests the daily rituals were elaborate and time-consuming. They were to recite all seventeen Gathas every morning, along with a modified version of the ancient *yasna* sacrifice, using both animals and the hallucinogenic substance known as *haoma*. Whereas formerly priests had extemporized the sacrificial formulas within certain patterns, Zoroaster seems to have established a set liturgy called the *Yasna haptanhaiti*, or "Seven-part worship." (The Younger Avesta, however, indicates that long after Zoroaster's time many priests continued to follow the older improvisatory tradition.) The formal liturgy begins with the intention to practice "good thoughts, good words, and good acts" – the threefold essence of Zoroastrian ethics. Mazda is then worshipped, along with four of the six other "good" *mainyu*s (called the Amesha Spentas, "Bounteous Immortals") which in the Zoroastrian reform were believed to emanate from him: Asha (truth), Vohu Manah ("good mind"), Kshathra (dominion), and Armaiti (devotion, obedience). The two others included in the divine heptad, Haurvatat (health, wholeness) and Ameretat (immortality), for some reason do not figure in the "seven-part worship."

The most important feast day of the Zoroastrian calendar was the spring equinox which marked the new year. This occasion, called Noruz ("New Day"), is still celebrated by Iranians and many neighboring peoples as well. It is a very old festival indeed, probably dating back into remote prehistory. In Zoroastrianism its symbolism of renewal was extended to include not only the resurgence of life every spring, but also to foreshadow the glorious future renewal of Frashokereti when evil would be forever overthrown. The annual festival has long been one of the most joyous occasions of the year for Iranians, and remains so today.

The Young Avesta further identifies six more festivals connected with the agricultural year – combined with Noruz, making seven altogether – which were celebrated by Zoroastrians from the earliest times. These seven holy days mirrored the seven aspects of the god-head expressed through Ahura Mazda and the Amesha Spentas, as well as the seven stages of original creation. Zoroastrians considered failure to observe each of these seven feast days to be a sin.

As with Noruz, Zoroastrianism absorbed and redefined a number of older festivals, just as other religions such as Christianity would do later. The result was sometimes slightly awkward, as in the case of an annual "all souls" ritual on the last night of the year. This appears to be of Indo-European origin, sharing its genealogy with Hallowe'en in Anglo-American tradition. There may have been some tensions connected with continuing to observe this ritual, and at the very least Zoroastrians were reminded to make offerings only to the departed souls (*fravashi*s) of those who had been good (*ashavan*). Over time the old ancestor cult seems to have crept back in, since the worship of *fravashi*s appears again in the later tradition.

Further persistence of religious rites "by popular demand" is evidenced in the Yashts of the Young Avesta. The Yashts, which are devotions directed at the whole range of *mainyu*s, were composed by Zoroastrian priests. Since priests earned their living by performing specific rites at the request of lay patrons – for success, for children, for a good harvest, or whatever – it can be imagined that the content and focus of the Yashts mainly represents their accommodation to the desires of the patrons and not necessarily those of the priests. As a result, the divine landscape of "beings worthy of worship" (*yazata*s) portrayed by the Yashts is considerably more "polytheistic" than that of the Mazda-focused Gathas of Zoroaster.

Zoroastrian priests also composed a set of purity regulations, called the *Videvdat*, literally, "laws against demons (*daeva*s)." Best known by its later name, the *Vendidad*, this compilation contains extensive instructions on maintaining the purity of earth, fire, and water. It prescribes capital punishment for anyone polluting a sacred fire, and advocates the killing of creatures believed to be "demonic," including insects, scorpions, and snakes, collectively known as *khrafstra*, which were seen as doing the evil work of Angra Mainyu.

The practice of consanguineous marriage, noted by the ancient Greeks and later ridiculed by the Jews, Christians, and Muslims, is held up as a virtuous deed in the Zoroastrian texts. Sibling marriages are no longer practiced today, but among Iranians of all religions there remains a preference for unions between first cousins.

## Religion under the Achaemenids

The first group of western Iranians to win mention in written sources of the Near East is the Medes, who were based in what is now north-central Iran south of the Alborz mountains. By the eighth century BCE it is likely that the Median priests had been won over to some form of Zoroastrian practice absorbed from the east, albeit one incorporating many local variations. During the early sixth century BCE Median power was challenged by another Iranian group from the southern region of Parsa, better known by its Greek form, Persia. Beginning in 549 BCE, Cyrus the Great eventually brought much of the Iranian plateau and neighboring Mesopotamia under his control, establishing the empire of the Achaemenids.

The Achaemenid sources are cuneiform inscriptions in a western Iranian dialect known as Old Persian – the direct ancestor of the modern Persian language. They are mainly in the form of royal decrees, declarations, and memorials, so the information they provide is somewhat limited. Although they nowhere mention Zoroaster, they do make frequent reference to Ahura Mazda and the "Mazda-worshiping religion," which they apparently used as an ideological tool to underpin the legitimacy of their conquests. Enemies, especially other Iranian tribes, are frequently disparaged as not worshiping Mazda, and occasionally the Achaemenids boast of having destroyed temples devoted to the worship of evil *daevas*. Around the time of Artaxerxes II (404–359 BCE) the royal inscriptions begin to mention Anahita, goddess of the waters (originally the Babylonian Ishtar, identified with Aphrodite of the Greeks and later Nanai among the Sogdians of Central Asia), alongside Ahura Mazda and Mithra. Indicative perhaps of Greek influence, Anahita is the first deity whom the Persians represented in statues.

It is the Greek sources that give the most detailed information about religion in Achaemenid times. Since the Persians were the main rivals to Greek power in the eastern Mediterranean region, the Greeks were very interested in learning about the culture of their opponents. Greek travelers to the Iranian world, such as Herodotus, were at least on some level acting as spies gone to report on the enemy. Interestingly, unlike the royal Achaemenid inscriptions, the Greek sources do mention Zoroaster as the main Persian prophet.

Herodotus states that in his time the Persians did not build temples to their gods, but performed their sacrifices "on every mountaintop" throughout the land. Eventually around the middle of the fourth century BCE the Persians did adopt the habit of building sacred shrines, presumably through the influence of their Babylonian and other Near Eastern neighbors. Most were in the form of mountaintop "fire temples" (*atash-gah*), though some were lavish buildings endowed and supported by the elites. Even today when traveling through Iran, it is possible to see the remains of these structures virtually everywhere, if one knows what to look for.

In the end it was the Greeks who prevailed in this stage of the long contest between East and West for control of the productive Near Eastern heartlands. Alexander of Macedon led his army into the Achaemenid capital of Persepolis, near modern Shiraz, and burned it almost to the ground in 332 BCE. For the next two centuries the bulk of Iranian territory, from the Mesopotamian plain to the borders of northwestern India, was under Greek control and the influence of Hellenistic culture.

Wherever they went, Greek armies built cities on the pattern of the Greek *polis*, complete with theaters, agoras (marketplaces), and temples to the Greek gods. These garrison towns were generally constructed adjacent to existing ones, so that Iranian lands became a mosaic of twin cities. (Russians and British did the same when they moved, respectively, into Central Asia and India during the late nineteenth century.) Excavations in the Oxus River region – what is now northern Afghanistan – have turned up evidence of a curious Greek-Iranian religious and cultural synthesis. Greek deities were identified with Iranian ones (Zeus with Ahura Mazda, Aphrodite with Anahita, and Apollo with Mithra, for example), and apparently in at least some cases Greeks and Iranians both worshiped their own gods in separate sections of the same temple. The practice evolved of representing Iranian deities in the Greek style, for example on coins. Greek-Iranian sites in western Iran include a shrine to Heracles/Verethraghna at Behistun, dated to 147 BCE, and a temple in Kurdistan at which both Artemis and Anahita were worshiped.

Eventually the Greek rulers in Iran, known as the "Seleucid" dynasty after one of Alexander's generals, were overthrown by an indigenous tribe, the Parni, who conquered Parthia in northeastern Iran (including what is now southern Turkmenistan). The Parthian, or Arsacid dynasty, would hold sway for almost four centuries, through the peak period of Roman empire-building. Indeed, the Parthians were the ones who halted that expansion to the east, blinding the Roman legions with their huge silk banners shimmering in the sunlight and antagonizing them with feigned cavalry retreats followed by volleys of over-the-shoulder arrows – the famed "Parthian shot."

The Parthians left few written records of their own, so it is difficult to know much about their religious beliefs and practices. It does appear, however, that in matters of religion they were highly tolerant, allowing their various subject peoples to carry on as they liked – provided, of course that they paid their taxes.

## Mithraism in the Roman world

Communities of Iranians existed throughout the eastern Mediterranean world from ancient times. Presumably most had established themselves there for purposes of trade. At times Egypt, Syria, and Anatolia had been under Achaemenid rule, which facilitated the settlement and flourishing of groups of Iranians. As these territories came under first Greek then Roman rule, Iranian expatriates continued to live there. Despite their minority status, many seem to have thrived, since Iranians are mentioned as underwriting the building of public structures and sponsoring athletes. The influence of Iranians was also felt in what would become a major movement in Roman society, particularly the army – namely, the cult of Mithra.

Mithraism was a mystery religion which centered on the notion of the soul's journey upward through seven spheres, symbolized by the devotee's passage through seven stages of secret initiation. The cult appears to have taken shape in the culturally mixed environment of Asia Minor during the first century BCE, and by the late first century CE it was widespread throughout the Roman Empire. Mithra was held to be the god of salvation, associated with the sun. Not insignificantly, perhaps, his birthday was celebrated on 25 December.

Devotees of Mithra congregated in a temple called the Mithraeum, which was meant to evoke the cave where according to myth Mithra had captured and killed the primordial bull – an echo of the bull sacrifice in ancient Iranian religion, but attributed to the evil Ahriman in Zoroastrianism. The cult, which was exclusively male, fostered camaraderie among its adherents, particularly soldiers who were frequently relocated from one post to another and thus lacked social roots.

With the adoption of Christianity as state religion of the Roman Empire in the early fourth century CE, followers of Mithraism along with other pagan cults and heterodox Christian groups were increasingly persecuted. Expatriate Iranians, meanwhile – presumably not numerous enough to appear a threat – seem to have been considered a sort of primitive curiosity and apparently kept themselves apart from mainstream society. Church correspondence of the late fourth century refers to them as "the nation of the Magians," a people who worship fire but lack both books and teachers, transmitting their traditions orally from one generation to the next. The picture is of an isolated and somewhat backward relic community.

Aspects of the Mithraic cult survived in heterodox sects of the Islamic period, notably in Kurdistan among the Yazidis (the name, while in its Arabized form has been interpreted as "devil-worshipers," may actually derive from *yazata*, i.e., "deity-worshipers") and the Ahl-e Haqq ("People of the Truth"). Both groups preserve the myth of a primordial contract – Mithra, it will be remembered, being the hypostatized deity of contracts – sealed by the sacrifice of a bull.

## The Sasanian state religion

Five hundred years after the fall of the Achaemenids, the Persians of the southwest once again rose to prominence, as armies led by the hereditary caretaker of a shrine to Anahita conquered the Parthian-held lands and founded the Sasanian dynasty in 224 CE. Anahita would remain the patron deity of the Sasanians throughout their four-hundred-year reign.

At first the Sasanian administration maintained the cultural policy of their Parthian predecessors, allowing their diverse subjects freedom in religious matters. Shortly, however, the Sasanian emperor

Ardeshir I, egged on perhaps by the Mazdaean priests seeking to centralize their own power, began authorizing the destruction of cult statues all over Iran and replacing them with sacred fires. The three greatest fires – Adur Burzen-Mehr in Parthia, Adur Gushnasp in Media, and Adur Farnbag in Pars – had probably been burning since Achaemenid times, but their shrines were greatly built up during the early Sasanian period. Ardeshir also called for the collection of religious teachings from throughout the empire, in an apparent early attempt to codify a state religion. This initiative, too, was probably instigated by his court priests.

Later sources attribute to Ardeshir the formal rejection of earlier policies of separating church and state. The Muslim writer Mas'udi describes religion and governance as something akin to siblings, echoing perhaps the Zurvanite view that Ormazd and Ahriman were brothers born of the remote Zurvan, god of time:

> Religion is the foundation of kingship, and kingship is the protector [of religion]. For whatever lacks a foundation must perish, and whatever lacks a protector disappears.[2]

This new policy may have been stimulated in part by a new challenge to the Mazdaean priesthood posed by the Parthian prophet Mani, founder of Manichaeaism. Born and raised in a hybrid Christian sect in Mesopotamia that was heavily influenced by Judaism and Gnosticism, Mani founded his own religion and eventually gained the ear of some members of the Sasanian royal family.

Mani's growing influence alarmed the Mazdaean priests. The chief magus, or *mobad*, of the royal court, Kerdir, spent years intriguing against his rival, finally succeeding in getting the emperor to arrest Mani and throw him into jail, where he died shortly afterward. But there were other threats as well; Christianity had won many converts in Iranian territory, fueled by the immigration of Christians fleeing persecution in the Roman lands and the forced transfer of Christian populations from conquered Roman territories. Kerdir campaigned vigorously against these and other foreign religions being practiced in Iranian lands, including Judaism, Mandaeism, Buddhism, and Brahmanism.

In the end the Mazdaean magi, led by Kerdir, managed to win for their faith the status of official religion of the Sasanian state. Thus empowered, they sent their representatives throughout the realm to enforce their own religious policies. At first these seem to have centered mainly on rituals associated with fire, water, the sun and moon, and cattle. Later, probably under Shapur II, the magi began writing down the sacred prayers and formulas that had been passed down orally since Zoroaster's time. The written form of the Avesta, including its Middle Persian translation and commentary called the Zand, dates from around the sixth century CE.

This was the formal beginning of the Zoroastrian textual tradition. While some of these previously oral texts, such as the Gathas, were surely very old, there was no real way to know the true origins of most of what would become a vast body of sacred literature. Some beliefs prominent in the Sasanian period appear to have been innovations, such as the elevation of Zurvan, the god of time and fate, to the position of original creator from whom both the god of good, Ormazd (Ahura Mazda), and the god of evil, Ahriman (Angra Mainyu) are born as brothers. In some variants of Iranian religion Zurvan takes over not only Ahura Mazda's position as supreme being, but also his association with light and the sun.

Among the rituals practiced during the Sasanian period, A. S. Melikian-Chirvani has cited wine libations, which at some earlier point had become a sublimation (as in the Christian eucharist) of sacrifices originally performed with blood. "From the earliest times," he speculates, "Persian literature echoes the ceremonial in which the wine would be poured out of animal-shaped vessels into crescent-shaped wine cups. Just as the wine was seen as liquid sunlight, red like sunset light, or liquid fire standing for sunlight, the crescent wine cups symbolized the moon. When filled with the 'body' of the sun, they signified the conjunction of the sun and the moon."[3] Although the significance in this regard of bull-shaped vessels is fairly obvious, far more preponderant is the occurrence of wine jugs shaped as ducks and other birds. The association of ducks with wine recurs later in Persian Sufi poetry.

With the establishment of Mazdaism as state church of the Sasanian regime, the mutual reliance of politicians and priests was likewise institutionalized. Nevertheless, over the subsequent three-and a-half-centuries of Sasanian rule, official attitudes towards religious orthodoxy varied depending on the moods of the emperor and changing political conditions. Perhaps the least tolerant of all the Sasanian emperors was Shapur II (r. 309–377). According to a later Zoroastrian text, the *Denkard*, early in his reign Shapur called together a consultation of representatives from the various religions present in his realm. At this event the primacy of the Mazdaean priests was confirmed. Shapur is reported to have declared, "Now that we have seen the faith as it truly is, we shall not tolerate anyone of false religion, and we shall be exceedingly zealous."[4] As indeed the record shows that he was.

From around 530 CE another threat to Zoroastrian supremacy appeared in the form of a popular movement led by a religious leader named Mazdak. The appeal of Mazdakism seems to have been one of social justice, indicating perhaps a worsening disparity between the elites – who included the Zoroastrian magi – and the impoverished masses. Mazdak preached a sort of proto-communism. He enjoined his followers to share their wealth equally, and, according to his detractors, their wives as well. The resulting social unrest led to outbreaks of rebellion and violence, until the recently enthroned Sasanian ruler Khosrow Anushirvan finally succeeded in having Mazdak arrested and executed. The Mazdakites went underground, but some of their ideas survived and reappeared in later rebellions such as that of Babak in the eighth century.

## The Islamization of Iran and Zoroastrian response

During the 640s the Sasanian regime, exhausted by endless wars with the eastern Romans (Byzantines) and heavily corrupted from within, succumbed to an unexpected invasion from a new power erupting out of the Arabian peninsula, the Muslims. Arabia, never (until the discovery of oil there in modern times) a highly prosperous or productive land, had always been on the fringes of civilization from the Iranian perspective. To be crushed by a people they had never taken seriously, and whom they viewed as being uncultured in the extreme, came as a huge shock to the proud Iranians, leaving a lasting trauma which arguably has not disappeared even today. The Persian national epic, the *Book of Kings* (*Shah-nameh*), which was redacted from diverse written (and possibly oral) traditions by Abo'l-Qasem Ferdowsi in the late tenth century, though compiled by a Muslim for

Muslims, treats the Arab conquest as the ultimate and culminating tragedy in the long heroic history of pre-Islamic Iran.

At first the Arabs, like many prior regimes, were content to live and let live as long as people acknowledged their rule and paid their taxes. But over time more and more Iranians who wished to join the ranks of the new ruling class chose to adopt the cultural norms and practices of their Arab overlords, which included the Islamic faith. It would seem that with the fall of the Sasanian ruling apparatus, as a state organization the Zoroastrian priesthood had lost a significant aspect of their strength.

It may be that in choosing to rely more on the support of the government than on that of the people, the Zoroastrian clergy had lost touch with the needs of the masses. (Many Iranians were converting to Christianity, Manichaeism, and other religions well before the arrival of the Arabs.) It is also the case that under Islamic law the children of mixed marriages – that is, a Muslim man marrying a non-Muslim woman – must be raised as Muslims, and that if one member of a non-Muslim family should convert to Islam then he would inherit the property of all of his non-Muslim relatives. Converts to Islam no longer had to pay the poll-tax (the *jizya*) levied on non-Muslims. Islamic law also governed the transactions of the market-place, to the general advantage of Muslim businessmen.

There is no way of knowing how many Iranian conversions came out of sincere belief in the superiority of the Qur'an and the example of the prophet Muhammad, and how many were merely opportunistic. In any event, within a few short centuries most of Iran's urban population – an estimated eighty percent by the year 1000 – had become Muslim. Conversion was slower in rural areas, but by the thirteenth century it appears that most rural Iranians were Muslims as well.

And yet throughout the Classical Islamic period Zoroastrian literary production flourished as never before, especially during the ninth and tenth centuries. While this may seem ironic at first glance, actually it makes perfect sense when one considers that writing is a kind of defense strategy. The first Zoroastrian books had been written down (albeit often based on much older oral literature) in the face of the threats posed by the worldviews of Manichaeaism and Christianity. The threat now was even greater, since Iranians were flocking in droves to the new religion and Zoroastrianism had lost its state support. Of this late literature the most important works are the quasi-historical *Denkard* ("Acts of the Faith") and a cosmogonic treatise called the *Bundahishn* ("the Primordial Creation"). At the same time, it is reported that many Zoroastrian books were permanently lost.

Although Muslim jurists in Iran mostly accorded Zoroastrians the protected status of a "people of the Book," in practice Muslim administrators and commoners alike often taunted and tormented Zoroastrians, whom they referred to derisively as "fire-worshipers" (*atash-parastan*) and "infidels" (*gabran*), in a variety of ways. Muslim officials were known to seize Zoroastrian property on very questionable legal grounds, or violate the sanctity of Zoroastrian sites such as in 861 when the Caliph Mutawakkil cut down a tree many believed to have been planted by Zoroaster himself. (The Caliph was assassinated soon after, which many Zoroastrians saw as an act of divine retribution.) Muslims would often attack and beat Zoroastrians in the street, or provoke them by torturing dogs – considered semi-sacred animals in Zoroastrianism but spurned as ritually unclean in Islam – a practice which continues in Iranian villages today.

## Zoroastrianism in India

By the ninth century it was clear that Islam had come to Iran to stay. With the majority of the population converted to this new faith, those who clung to the old religion were an embattled minority. Some chose exile, migrating to the more tolerant climate of western India. The community of Zoroastrian refugees in India, where they came to be known as Parsees ("Persians"), established itself mainly in the region of Gujarat by around 936 CE, where they remain a presence to this day.

Through the centuries contacts between Zoroastrians in Iran and India have been intermittent. During the nineteenth century these contacts were revived with British support. A Society for the Amelioration of the Conditions of the Zoroastrians in Persia was founded in Bombay in 1854. The Society sent a Parsee agent by the name of Manekji Limji Hataria to Iran to assess the condition of Zoroastrian communities there, which he found to be abysmal. Manekji established schools in Zoroastrian communities and worked

for the repeal of the *jizya*, the poll tax levied on Zoroastrians as a
non-Muslim community. Through the efforts of the Society and with
the help of British pressure on the Iranian government, the tax was
repealed in 1882.

Although today there are still small numbers of Zoroastrians in
Iran – mainly in the remote desert areas of Yazd and Kerman – the
largest population of Zoroastrians in the world is in the city of Bombay
(Mumbai), and there are many in Delhi and other Indian cities as
well. They tend to be well-to-do, and are influential in Indian affairs
well out of proportion to their small numbers. The Tata Corporation,
for example, one of India's largest companies, is Parsee-owned. The
husband of former Prime Minister Indira Gandhi (no relation to the
Mahatma) was from a well-known Parsee family.

## Zoroastrians in modern Iran

After the abolition of the poll tax in 1882 the economic conditions
of Iranian Zoroastrians began to improve. Many moved to Tehran
where they saw increased opportunities and, in the cosmopolitan environment of the capital, suffered less from daily acts of bigotry on
the part of Muslims. After Iran's first parliament was established in
1906 one seat was allocated to a Zoroastrian representative.

In 1908 Tehran's growing Zoroastrian community established
a sacred fire temple, which exists today on a quiet street near the
center of the city. From 1925 the new king, Reza Shah Pahlavi,
promoted a secular nationalist policy (in emulation of his Turkish
neighbor Kemal Ataturk) which worked in some ways to the benefit
of Iran's Zoroastrians. During Reza Shah's reign pre-Islamic Iranian
culture was elevated as being more truly "Persian" than Islam, and
in the minds of some Iranians this brought a new respect for
Zoroastrianism. Intellectuals such as Sadeq Hedayat (1903–1951),
arguably Iran's greatest novelist, developed a keen interest in the literature of the Sasanian period, and very small numbers of Muslim
Iranians even began to "convert back" to Zoroastrianism as being
a more authentically Iranian form of religion.

As Zoroastrians became exposed to modernist ideas, some leading
members of the community, such as parliamentary deputy Keikhosrow
Shahrokh, pushed for reforming certain aspects of religious practice.

The exposure of corpses, for example, was argued to be a post-Zoroaster innovation, and by the 1960s was abandoned as unhygienic.

In addition to India, there are long-established Parsee communities in Pakistan, Sri Lanka, Hong Kong, and Singapore. With the Iranian diaspora entering a new phase in the second half of the twentieth century, Iranian Zoroastrian communities grew up in places like London, Toronto, and Los Angeles. The first World Zoroastrian Congress was held in 1960 in Tehran. Subsequent conferences have been held in Iran, India, and the United States.

There are now Zoroastrian cultural organizations in a number of countries. The World Zoroastrian Organisation in London, the Zarathushtrian Assembly of California, and others are now actively supporting Zoroastrian communities and promoting Zoroastrian teachings both locally and worldwide. A Zoroastrian virtual university, Spenta University, has been set up in Los Angeles and offers on-line programs leading to graduate degrees in the United States, Iran, India, Italy, Switzerland, Brazil, Australia, and Venezuela. In Iran, the Zoroastrians of Shiraz maintain an informational website in both English and Persian. In a sense, Zoroastrianism, one of the world's oldest religions, has only recently become a world religion.

## Zoroastrianism's contributions to other religions

Much of what has been described in this chapter as "the basics" of Zoroastrianism will no doubt seem familiar to many readers. What may not be apparent is that these widespread beliefs and practices appeared in Zoroastrianism first, and only later in other religions. The concept of an all-powerful Creator god who is purely good, the personification of evil in an opposing being, the resurrection of the body after death, the judgment of the dead on the basis of their deeds while living, the existence of a heavenly paradise for the good and a hell of damnation for the evil, the expectation of a savior and a final cataclysmic battle in which good will ultimately triumph, as well as a universe populated by angels and demons, are all ideas that other religions acquired either directly or indirectly from Zoroastrianism.

Other notions, such as the possibility of an individual as opposed to communal relationship to the divine, the superiority of one faith over all others, the emphasis on right belief and not just practice, and a professed adherence not only to a single deity but also to a particular prophet, may have originated with Zoroaster as well. For the first time we hear of a religion being actively spread by missionaries, who are sometimes persecuted or killed for their efforts. How all these ideas and influences found their way into later traditions will be explored in the following chapters.

# 3

# JUDAISM

It can rightly be said that the Jewish diaspora, spanning twenty-seven centuries, begins in Iran. In fact, it has been argued that Iran is second only to Israel in historical importance for the Jews.[1] The religious and cultural tradition now known as Judaism underwent one of its most radical transformations as a result of contact with Iranians. This influence, which is felt in the later development of Christianity and Islam, reverberates throughout the cultures of more than half the world today.

Modern Judaism is largely a product of the Talmudic period – that is, the first through the sixth centuries of the Common Era. But of course, the roots of Judaism are much older. The traditional chronology, which is based on the genealogies of the Hebrew Bible, goes back to a purported date of Creation in 3750 BCE. Abraham, who is considered by Jews (and, for that matter, by Muslims as well) to be the founder of their religion, may have lived sometime around the eighteenth century BCE. But as is the case with all human cultures, the history of Judaism is a dynamic one, sometimes undergoing dramatic changes and developments. The Jewish faith as practiced today scarcely resembles the sacrificial religion of ancient times, and yet a distinct thread of continuity connects them through time and space.

## The beginnings of diaspora

One of the watershed periods of Jewish history is the reign of King David in the tenth century BCE, when the Israelites controlled a kingdom between the Sea of Galilee and the Dead Sea in the region of Palestine. Following the reign of David's son Solomon, the Israelite state split into two kingdoms, the northern kingdom of Israel and the southern kingdom of Judea. Although in the Bible these kingdoms are naturally treated as the center of the world – which, for Israelites, they were – from the perspective of the great contemporary civilizations based in the Nile valley and Mesopotamia, Palestine was hardly more than a small, remote place of little economic value or strategic importance. Not surprisingly, the Israelites do not figure prominently in the records of their larger imperial neighbors.

We do know from both Hebrew and Mesopotamian sources that the northern kingdom of Israel was overrun by the armies of Assyria in the 720s BCE. It was the custom of the Assyrians (who were a Semitic people) to uproot the survivors in all the regions they conquered, and resettle them elsewhere within their empire. The Bible states in the Second Book of Kings (18:11) that Israelites were sent to live in "Halah and Habor by the River Gozan and in the cities of the Medes" – that is, in western and northern Iran. This can be taken as evidence for an Israelite presence in Iran from the eighth century BCE at the latest. Some may have gone even further east. There is a legend among the Pushtuns of modern Afghanistan that they are themselves descended from the ten "lost" tribes of Israel, and the story may have some historical substance. Although most of the Pushtuns converted to Islam many centuries ago, small Jewish communities survived in Afghanistan into the 1990s.

In 586 BCE the southern kingdom of Judea succumbed as well, this time to the Babylonians (who were also Semitic) under King Nebuchadnezzar. The Babylonian soldiers utterly destroyed the Judean capital, Jerusalem, including the Temple built in the time of King Solomon, which was the center of the Israelites' sacrificial religion. In a sense, by destroying the Temple the Babylonians rendered the religious life of the Israelites non-functional, since the required sacrifice could only be performed there.

Like the Assyrians, the Babylonians had a policy of resettling conquered peoples. The Bible describes this process and its consequences from the point of view of the Israelites, whose Babylonian captivity is interpreted as Yahweh's punishment for their failure to keep the covenant established through Moses on Mount Sinai.

A few decades later, in 539 BCE, the armies of a new power to the east, the Achaemenids of Parsa in southwestern Iran, entered Babylon and liberated all the captive peoples, Israelites included. While, again, it is important to keep a sense of perspective here – to the Persians, the Israelites cannot have seemed any different from any other captive group – the biblical version of events places the Hebrew god at the center of this great historical occasion, describing the Persian emperor Cyrus as "God's anointed" who has been brought for the purpose of saving the Israelites (Isaiah 44:25–28 and 45:1–4). In other words, whereas to most peoples of the time Cyrus was simply the latest in a long line of empire-builders, seeking his own glory above all else, in the Bible his success is seen as a sign of the glory of God. It is interesting that of all the foreign rulers mentioned in the Hebrew Bible, only Cyrus is described in positive terms.

The Achaemenid conquest represented the beginning of Iranian influence in Mesopotamia. This was a region which had long possessed an enormous diversity of ethnicities, languages, and cultures (think "Tower of Babel"), though Semitic peoples predominated. When Cyrus liberated the captive peoples of Babylon he granted them what might be described today as "citizenship" in his empire and the freedom to settle anywhere they would choose. At the time few Israelites felt the desire to return to their ruined homeland. Instead, many remained in Babylon as free citizens, while others sought new lives elsewhere. (The Temple in Jerusalem was not rebuilt until the following century, with Persian assistance.) Significant numbers appear to have gone to live in the cities of the Iranian plateau, perhaps making contact with Israelites already living there from Assyrian times. Hence the observation that "the diaspora begins in Iran."

From the beginning of the diaspora twenty-seven centuries ago, the dispersed Israelites (the term "Jew," in its Greek form *iudaios*, or "Judean," doesn't appear until the third century BCE) maintained connections with family and friends in other locations that formed the basis of long-distance trade networks. Israelites likely played a role in the silk trade which linked China to the West.

These diaspora networks served not only to sustain family ties and business contacts, but also as conduits for goods and ideas. Thus, the experiences and achievements of one community could be easily transmitted over time to other related communities far away. Since in Achaemenid times the Persian Empire of which the Israelites were citizens stretched from Egypt and Greece to the borders of China and India, different Israelite groups found themselves living in very diverse cultural and physical environments. Of course Iranians settled in all of these areas too, with the result that the whole range of products and technologies, lifestyle and customs, art forms and philosophies could travel readily from one locale to another within this far-flung and cosmopolitan empire. Among the actual transmitters of all these cultural artifacts, the ancestors of Iranian Jews were prominent.

At the same time, the influences absorbed from Iranian culture by the Israelites themselves were enormous. In order to assess the extent of these influences, it is necessary to consider the religio-cultural system of the Israelites prior to their encounter with Iranians.

## The influence of Iranian ideas

The religion of the ancient Israelites could be characterized in one sense as a "Yahweh-cult." That is, they were a group distinguished from neighboring Semitic tribes mainly by their adherence to a particular God, Yahweh, who established a covenant with them through Moses on Mount Sinai (probably some time in the thirteenth century BCE). That is, the role of Moses among the Israelites can be seen as analogous to that of Zoroaster among the Iranians, in that they both elevated a god already existing within the pantheon of their peoples to a position of supremacy.

In neither case are we dealing with monotheism strictly speaking. The First Commandment delivered on Mount Sinai is "Thou shalt have no other gods before me," an implicit admission that other gods exist. Likewise, Zoroaster merely demoted some gods to the level of servants or emanations of Ahura Mazda, and others, like the *daeva*s, to the status of demons. As in the Iranian world, the Israelite holy texts were memorized and passed on by the priestly class who alone knew the correct sacrificial formulas. And just as with the Avesta and the Rig Veda, by the time these texts were written down the sacred language – Hebrew in this case – was no longer spoken or perhaps even fully understood by the people, who had adopted regional vernaculars.

But there are many ways in which the Israelite vision of the universe and their place in it differed dramatically from that of the Iranians. The Israelites seem to have had little clear notion of the afterlife, assuming that souls merely went to reside in a murky underworld known as Sheol. They lacked the elaborate angelology and demonology of the Iranians, and they had no notion of "the devil," only the gods of others whom the Israelites were forbidden to worship (but whom, as the biblical prophets endlessly complain, they often did anyway). The Israelites' conception of time, like most ancient peoples, was cyclical, based on the seasons and the agricultural year. The linear time and apocalyptic eschatology described in Zoroaster's cosmos is absent from the pre-Babylonian Israelite worldview. The Israelite sense of ethics was based on the community, rather than on the individual. Whereas the Hebrew biblical tradition speaks of Yahweh's covenant with a people and collective guilt and punishment, Zoroaster's vision focuses on personal responsibility for choosing good over evil.

The apocalypticism of biblical prophets such as Daniel dates from the post-Babylonian period after Israelites had come into contact with Iranian ideas. The concept of a messiah (literally, "anointed one") who will come to save the righteous at the end of time would seem to derive from the Iranian belief in the Saoshyant. The figure of *ha-Satan*, literally "the accuser," appears no earlier than in the Book of Job, which was composed in the post-exilic period as well. Thus, the Satan reviled by Christians and Muslims alike clearly evolved from the Zoroastrian evil deity, Ahriman, a notion most likely transmitted to the Semitic world by the Jews of Iran.

The Book of Esther is entirely set in Iran, being the story of a Jewish orphan girl, Hadassah (Esther), who marries the Persian ruler and becomes queen. Properly mindful of her origins, she uses her power and status to save her people from a purge instigated by the jealous prime minister Haman, who maliciously informs the king that the Jews are a people "whose laws are different from those of any other people and who do not obey the king's laws" (3:8).

The final section of the Book of Esther describes how the Jewish festival of Purim came into being:

> For Haman son of Hammedatha the Agagite, the foe of all the Jews, had plotted to destroy the Jews, and had cast *pur* – that is, the lot – with intent to crush and exterminate them. But when [Esther] came before the king, he commanded: "With the promulgation of this decree, let the evil plot, which he had devised against the Jews, recoil on his own head!" So they impaled him and his sons on the stake. For that reason these days were named Purim, after *pur*.
>
> In view, then, of all the instructions in the said letter and of what they had experienced in that matter and what had befallen them, the Jews undertook and irrevocably obligated themselves and their descendants, and all who might join them, to observe these two days in the manner prescribed and at the proper time each year. Consequently, these days are recalled and observed in every generation: by every family, every province, and every city. And these days of Purim shall never cease among the Jews, and the memory of them shall never perish among their descendants.[2]

In reality the Jewish Purim seems to have been adapted from the Iranian springtime celebration of Fravardigan, much as European Christians would later transform the pagan Yule into Christmas. Esther and her adoptive father, Mordecai, are said to have been buried in the Iranian city of Hamadan, where their tombs have long been a destination of Jewish pilgrims who wish to honor their memory. The tomb of the prophet Daniel is also believed to be in Iran, in the southwestern city of Shush (Susa).

## The influence of Hellenism

The language chosen by the Achaemenids to rule their western provinces was Aramaic, which was the lingua franca of most Semitic peoples including the Jews. In the last third of the fourth century BCE, however, Alexander of Macedon led his armies from Greece into Egypt, Persia, Central Asia, and even northwestern India, bringing all of the Achaemenid-ruled lands under his control and opening up the way for centuries of Greek influence to penetrate throughout the region. The effects of Greek culture, called "Hellenism" (after Hellas, the ancient name for Greece) took the form of language, philosophy, and the arts, among other things.

Among the cities where Jews lived, Alexandria in Egypt (one of many cities founded by the conqueror and named after himself) came to rival Babylon both in terms of overall Jewish population and as a center for Jewish culture. The first translation of the Hebrew Bible, known as the Septuagint (from "seventy," the number of translators supposedly involved), was made into Greek by Alexandrian Jews, making the holy scriptures available for the first time to a non-priestly audience.

Hellenized Jews, connected by trade networks with Jewish communities in Iran, acted as cultural filters transforming and transmitting Iranian stories and concepts throughout the eastern Mediterranean world. Fueled by Iranian eschatologies, Jewish messianic and apocalyptic movements arose in Mesopotamia and elsewhere. One typical end-of-the-world tale, originally from Parthia in eastern Iran, was rewritten into Greek by a Jewish author and circulated as *The Oracles of Hystaspes* (Vishtaspa), purporting to be an ancient Iranian prophecy foretelling the destruction of Jerusalem. The Greek work in turn served as a major influence on the later Christian Book of Revelation.

Around two thousand years ago, the blending of Greek, Semitic, and Iranian elements also constituted the foundation for an emerging mystical movement which came to be known as Gnosticism. Gnostics – literally, "those who know" – often symbolized their spiritual rebirth by undergoing ritual baptism, a practice possibly evolved out of the "trial by water" prevalent among the ancient Iranians. Various messianic and Gnostic-baptist sects emerged all throughout the Near East, especially in Mesopotamia. Some of these groups apparently considered themselves Jewish, further complicating existing claims to authority between the hereditary Jewish priests and the scholarly rabbis.

## The rabbinic period

The translation of the Bible into Greek symbolized a sort of democratization of the Jewish tradition, in the sense that the traditional monopoly of priests over the religious practice of the Israelites could now be accessed by anyone literate in Greek. The strongest claim of the priests, once their unique possession of the sacred texts was taken away from them, was that they alone could perform the prescribed sacrifice on which the Hebrew religion was based at the Temple in Jerusalem. However, since from the sixth century BCE most Jews lived outside Palestine, they began to derive their own metaphorical means of practicing their religion, congregating in synagogues and following interpretations of the holy texts made by non-priestly scholars, called rabbis.

In the year 70 CE, following a Jewish revolt in Palestine, the Roman army destroyed Jerusalem and razed the Temple, just as the Babylonians had done six centuries earlier. This time the Temple was not rebuilt. Since the ritual sacrifice could not be performed elsewhere than at the Temple in Jerusalem, the priests were at last deprived of their remaining power, leaving the rabbis as the main source of spiritual guidance for Jews everywhere.

The rabbis were not the only group vying for this authority, however. Various sects followed leaders and texts of their own, challenging the rabbinical interpretations. The most significant such sect, of course, was the Christians, whose interpretation of biblical prophecies and laws radically differed from that of the rabbis. Since many of the Gnostic and apocalyptic sects mentioned earlier also rejected the rabbis' supremacy, it became increasingly necessary for the rabbis to establish a tradition that they could claim as normative for all Jews.

One specific claim the rabbis had been making since at least the third century BCE was that they had received a large body of revelation handed down orally since the time of Moses, what they called "the oral Torah," which supplemented and exceeded in quantity the written Torah of the priests. Following the model of the Christians, and eventually the Manichaeans and Zoroastrians, the rabbis began to write down the oral Torah as a text they called the Mishnah. They developed a highly sophisticated form of scholarly debate over the meanings and applications of this text, which in turn they wrote down as a commentary on the Mishnah called the Gemara. Taken together, the Mishnah and its commentary came to constitute what Jews now know as the Talmud, which is the basis for modern Judaism.

This process, which began in the third century CE and lasted until the end of the fifth, occurred in two locations, resulting in two Talmuds. The first, completed by around 400 CE, was the work of scholars in the Galilee region and is known as the Palestinian Talmud. The second, longer work, completed by 600, was compiled in Babylon, which was still the main center of Jewish culture, and is referred to as the Babylonian Talmud. Since Babylon was a part of the Iranian world and, as one scholar has noted, "Iranian cultural influences are manifest" in it, the Babylonian Talmud might without too much exaggeration be called an "Iranian Talmud."[3] Many of these influences were negative ones, however, as the rabbis sought to maintain community identity through the discouraging of interactions between Jews and non-Jews in a highly cosmopolitan environment.

Rabbis and magi, along with religious leaders of other Babylonian communities, tended to be valued by the general population in terms of their effectiveness with spells and incantations, and people would often consult whichever figures they believed most skilled in this regard whatever their religious affiliation. Like the magi, the rabbis had to wage ongoing battles against syncretism in an effort to keep the religious identities of their communities distinct. The rabbis were also concerned by conversions of Jews to Christianity, especially since many Jewish-Christians continued to live in Jewish society and even worshipped in synagogues.

During most of the Talmudic period Babylonia was under the control of the Sasanian Persian dynasty, which had made Zoroastrianism the official state religion. A stone inscription left by the magus Kerdir in the third century boasts of punishing all those who refused to worship Ahura Mazda, including the Jews. But the Sasanians' treatment of non-Zoroastrian communities varied according to time and circumstance.

For example, according to some stories in the Talmud, the Sasanian ruler Yazdigerd I (r. 399–421) had close relations with a number of rabbis and was generally helpful to Jewish communities in Esfahan and elsewhere.[4] On the other hand, by the time of Yazdigerd II (r. 439–57) the agitations of Jewish messianists seem to have aroused the concern of the Sasanian government, who outlawed the observation of the Sabbath, closed Jewish schools, and executed Jewish leaders. The Jews of Esfahan responded by killing two

Zoroastrian priests, and in turn the Sasanians massacred much of the city's Jewish population.

## The coming of Islam

By the time Arab armies conquered the Sasanian empire in the 640s of the Common Era, Jews may have constituted the majority in some parts of Mesopotamia. This region would become the heartland of the Islamic caliphate, and it seems likely that many converts to Islam there had originally been Jews. Certainly the influence of Jewish traditions on the emerging Islamic civilization is very clear.

It is surely no accident that the Islamic legal code, the *shari'a*, so closely resembles that of the Talmudic tradition, as does the process by which Muslim scholars debated and derived it. The *shari'a* was a product mainly of the heavily Persianized Islamic culture of Baghdad and elsewhere in Mesopotamia, where the majority of Muslims came from Jewish or Christian backgrounds. Probably many of the lawyers who codified the *shari'a* were themselves descended from Jews, and Arab scholars as well as Iranian converts from Zoroastrianism or Buddhism learned to use the rabbis' techniques of argumentation and scholarship. In the cosmopolitan atmosphere of the High Caliphate, furthermore, Jewish and Christian scholars regularly mixed and debated with their Muslim counterparts. The Jewish academies at Pumbedita and Sura in Babylonia continued to flourish well into the Muslim period.

Many Jewish physicians, mathematicians, and astronomers found employment at the court of the Muslim Caliph. Jewish scholars were prominent among those translating works of classical science and philosophy from Greek into Arabic. Owing to their international connections they were sometimes used as ambassadors. Though Jews, like Christians and other non-Muslims, were required to wear distinctive clothing and were subject to numerous restrictions, for the most part they were left to run their own affairs. Jewish communities throughout the Muslim world were represented by the *Resh galuta*, the Exilarch at Baghdad, who was answerable on their behalf and responsible for collecting and passing on taxes to the Caliphal government.

Jewish trade networks flourished during the early Islamic period, extending from the Mediterranean and northern Europe as far as India and China. It is interesting to note that although the written Persian language was replaced by Arabic following the Muslim conquests, Jews played a role in its reemergence in the eastern Iranian world two centuries later. A Jewish merchant's letter from the eighth century and found in the Tarim desert of what is now western China is the oldest known written example of the now Arabized so-called "New Persian" language, which is the basis of standard Persian today.

## Radical Jewish resistance movements

Times of crisis tend to produce radical movements and ideas, and the mass conversions of Jews to Islam constituted a crisis for Jewish communities everywhere. In Iran, one such movement in the 740s rallied around a figure by the name of Abu Isa Esfahani, whose followers believed him to be the promised messiah. They practiced vegetarianism – a possible influence from Manichaeism which was then widespread – and their approach was characterized by an attitude of mourning which, though it ostensibly centered on the loss of the Temple in Jerusalem, would seem to echo the tragic ethos of Shi'i Islam, a popular underground movement at the time. At its peak Abu Isa's sect counted upwards of ten thousand followers, and it persisted for at least several centuries.

Around the same time and place, another Iranian Jewish movement arose in opposition to the authority of the rabbis. The Karaites, as they were known, rejected the Talmudic laws and advocated the observance only of laws present in the original Torah. They too adopted an attitude of mourning reminiscent of the Shi'ite Muslims, banning the Sabbath and all other joyous Jewish holidays. The Karaites observed a fast which resembled the Islamic Ramadan. Intellectually, they practiced a philosophical rationality similar to that of the Muslim Mu'tazilites. The Karaite philosophy played a role in the conversion to Judaism of the Turkish Khazar rulers of the north Caspian region in the mid-eighth century.

A few decades later, in the 830s, an Iranian Jew by the name of Abu Amran led a sect which rejected the belief in a bodily resurrection (which, it will be remembered, was an Iranian idea in the first place, and not a Hebrew one). His followers referred to him as "the Iranian Moses."

In the eastern Iranian city of Balkh a Jewish scholar by the name of Hiwi wrote the first commentary on the Bible from the standpoint of literary criticism. Though his work is lost (or destroyed), his "Two Hundred Criticisms" are known through the refutations of the tenth-century rabbi Saadia Gaon.

By the tenth century the center of Jewish learning had moved from Babylonia to Andalusia (Spain). Nevertheless, as late as the twelfth century messianic figures were still appearing in Iranian Jewish communities. Beginning in 1121 a charismatic individual from the region of Azerbaijan by the name of David al-Ruy, who was apparently a skilled magician, tried to assemble a Jewish army to retake Jerusalem, which was then in the hands of the Christian Franks. The movement was unsuccessful, but David's example continued to inspire later Jewish groups.

## Iranian Jews in the Mongol period

With the relocation of Jewish culture's center of gravity to Spain, eastern Jews became somewhat marginalized. Even so, significant Jewish communities persisted throughout the Muslim world and beyond. Jews continued to play important roles in trade, establishing networks all across Asia. Though the origins of the Jewish community in China (which vanished only as late as the 1950s) cannot be dated or traced with any certainty, it seems likely that they came originally from Iran. Silk Road cities such as Samarkand and Bukhara had large Jewish quarters, though in recent times most Central Asian Jews have migrated to Israel.

When the Mongol armies erupted out of Inner Asia and took control of much of Eurasia throughout the thirteenth century, one of their major aims was to control the long-distance trade routes – what might be called in modern-day parlance "the elimination of trade barriers." Since Iranian Jewish businessmen were prominent players in the trade networks which linked the Mediterranean world with China, and since Jewish communities were too small to constitute a political threat, some Jews were able to benefit from Mongol patronage and attain important commercial and political positions.

In the 1280s, for example, a Jewish physician by the name of Mordecai gained the attention of the Mongol governor of Tabriz,

Arghun Khan, who appointed him prime minister over all of Iran. Though Mordecai had ostensibly become a Muslim, earning the title Sa'd al-Dawla, or "fortune of the State," the fact that Muslim sources refer to him as "the Jewish vizier" suggests a mainly pragmatic conversion. Once in power Sa'd al-Dawla appointed many of his Jewish relatives to governorships throughout the realm, causing intense resentment among the Muslims. Rumors began to circulate that he intended to take Jerusalem (echoes of David al-Ruy) and give it back to the Jews, and turn the *ka'aba* in Mecca into an idol temple. In 1291 he was executed.

Only a few years later, however, in 1298, another Jewish physician rose to the position of prime minister in Tabriz. Again a convert to Islam, he is known only by his Muslim name Rashid al-din Fazlullah. Rashid al-din wrote books on medicine and other subjects, and is best known as the author of the encyclopedic world history *Jami' al-tawarikh* ("Collection of Histories"), which was commissioned by the Mongol court.

An able administrator, Rashid al-din reformed the fiscal, commercial, legal, and postal systems of the Mongol state in Iran. He oversaw the construction of roads and the strengthening of public security. Like his predecessor, however, his power won him many enemies and in 1318 he too was executed as a result of intrigues at court. The downfalls of both Jewish premiers were followed by pogroms against Jews. Rashid al-din's son, Ghiyas al-din Muhammad, eventually succeeded him, but in 1337 he was executed as well.

Never again would the Jews of Iran have the benefit of powerful benefactors in government. The latter half of the fourteenth century saw the rise of Tamerlane (*Timur-e Lang*, "Lame Timur" on account of a childhood accident), a Central Asian Turk who saw himself as a conqueror in the mold of Chinggis Khan but with the religious zeal of a ruthless Islamic reformer. He championed mainstream Sunni Islam against enemies of all kinds whom he would accuse of heresy, and the Jews were not spared his "ethnic cleansing." According to one story, Tamerlane was riding past a synagogue in Esfahan, when the chanting from within startled his horse and threw the emperor. Furious, he ordered the massacre of the entire congregation. Habib Levy estimates that some 350,000 Iranian Jews were killed, converted, or fled Iran during Tamerlane's rule.[5]

Iran's best-known Jewish poet, Shahin of Shiraz, flourished during the Mongol rule in the early fourteenth century. Shahin is famous for having rendered a number of the books of the Hebrew Bible into Persian verse, including much of the Torah (that is, the first five books, otherwise known as the Pentateuch) and the books of Job, Esther, and Ezra. His treatments often mirror those of Muslim poets drawing on the same themes, such as the fall of the angel Azazel (the future Satan) from heaven after refusing to bow down before Adam – a popular story among Sufis – or that of the Joseph story, which in Shahin's version bears as much resemblance to the Qur'anic account as it does to the biblical version.

A blending of Iranian and Jewish identities characterizes much of Judeo-Persian literature. The seventeenth-century writer Babai son of Lutf, best known for his accounts of persecution suffered by Esfahan's Jews, also wrote poetry in which he incorporated Iranian themes into Jewish subjects, as in the following verse in praise of the prophet Elijah:

> Peacock of Mercy's oasis
> Simorgh of the tower of gnosis
> Toll gatherer on the road to finis
> O Elijah, take my hand.[6]

The peacock is a motif imported from the Persian poetry of India, whereas the Simorgh is a mythical bird from ancient Iranian legends. The term translated as "gnosis" is *ma'rifa*, a central theme in Sufism. Later in the same poem Babai refers to Elijah as the *mahdi*, or Islamic messiah, and "our intercessor," a role attributed in popular Islam to Muhammad. Such examples vividly illustrate the degree to which writers like Babai felt both Iranian and Jewish.

## The Safavid period

A Turkish group led by the Safavi family of Ardebil in Azerbaijan conquered Iran in 1501 and began a century-long process of forcing the country's Muslims, most of whom were Sunnis, to the Shi'i branch of Islam. Although the brunt of the Safavids' ideological force was directed at Sunni Muslims, the Shi'ite clerics who supported the government considered Jews to be ritually unclean. This attitude on the part of Iran's Shi'ite Muslims, which extended to Christians and Zoroastrians as well, intensified the marginalization of the Jewish communities all throughout Iran. Non-Muslims were required to wear distinctive headgear and clothing, and Shi'ite clerics occasionally ordered the public burning of Hebrew books.

As a result of tensions between the Safavids and the Sunni Ottomans who controlled Mesopotamia, relations between Iranian Jewish communities and those further west were dramatically reduced. Many Jews converted to Islam during this period, at least outwardly, though like the members of other religious minority communities some of them continued to practice their original faith in private. This was in contrast to the situation in the Ottoman world, where Sephardic Jews expelled from Spain had been welcomed and where Jewish communities thrived.

In the middle of the seventeenth century Jews throughout the Middle East were roused by an Ottoman Jew, Shabbatai Zevi, who claimed that he was the promised messiah. In response to this development, the Safavid ruler Shah Abbas II issued a decree that all Jews under his rule must convert to Islam. Many chose to emigrate instead, mainly to the Ottoman lands. Those who remained in Iran were subject to all manner of discriminatory restrictions and lived under the constant threat of harassment and torture. One night in 1658 the Jews of Esfahan were summarily ordered to move outside the city walls.

The Safavid dynasty was brought to an end when the Afghan tribals conquered Esfahan in 1722. The Afghans, who were Sunnis, continued the policy of forcing Iranian Jews to convert to Islam. Under the Afsharid dynasty established by Nader Khan in 1732, the subsequent Zand dynasty during the second half of the eighteenth century, and the Qajars throughout the nineteenth, Iran's dwindling Jewish communities were characterized mainly by their poverty and marginal status. Frequent riots and other forms of civil unrest which marked the reign of the weak Qajars often resulted in unruly mobs looting Jewish shops and attacking Jews.

The revolutionary Babi movement of the 1840s, led by a self-proclaimed prophet who extended the promise of equal consideration to Jews, attracted a small number of Jewish followers. Although the Babis were ruthlessly crushed following their assassination attempt on the Qajar king Naser al-Din in 1852, a remnant of the movement emerged a decade later as the newly pacifist Baha'is. Among the converts to this new world faith were many Iranian Jews. During the latter half of the nineteenth century European missionaries, who were prohibited from proselytizing among Iran's Muslims, also won converts from Judaism.

From the 1870s European Jews began to take an interest in the plight of Iranian Jewry. In 1898 the Paris-based Alliance Israelite Universelle opened a school in Tehran, followed by others in different parts of the country. The Jews were granted one seat in Iran's new parliament following the Constitutional Revolution of 1906, although their "representative" was a Muslim, and therefore really more of an ombudsman.

Reza Shah Pahlavi's pro-German policies of the 1930s created an uncomfortable climate for Iranian Jews, who were often vilified in the press. With the founding of the state of Israel in 1948 over one third of Iran's Jews emigrated there. Many settled in Jaffa, where today one can often hear Persian spoken in the shops and streets.

Under Mohammad Reza Shah Pahlavi in the 1950s and 1960s, the situation of Iran's remaining Jews improved markedly. The Shah established close relations with Israel, which became a major ally. Jewish children were allowed to attend Hebrew schools, and Jews figured prominently in Iranian academia and medicine. All of these factors led to a severe backlash after the 1979 revolution, however, since Jews were seen by the resurgent Islamists as being simultaneously in league with a corrupt king and an illegitimate foreign state.

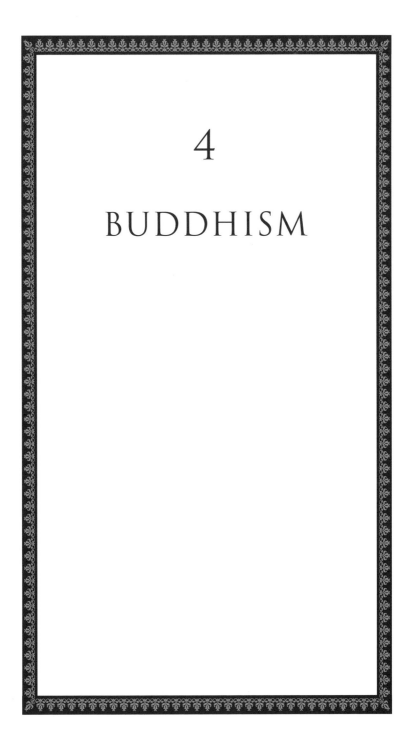

4

# BUDDHISM

The evidence and documentation for Iranian Buddhism is unfortunately more sparse and fragmentary than for any of Iran's other historical religions. This is due in part at least to the fact that Buddhism is the only once-prevalent religion to have disappeared entirely from Iran, a disappearance that was complete by as much as a thousand years ago. As a result, knowledge about Iran's relationship to this major world religion is limited mainly to inferences and suppositions based on inexplicit or second-hand sources. Nevertheless, it is clear that for a number of centuries, a huge proportion of the Iranian population practiced Buddhism, especially in the east, and it is equally apparent that Iranian Buddhists infused the tradition with a large number of distinctly Iranian ideas which remain present especially in Mahayana Buddhism today.

Buddhism arose in northern India sometime around the fifth century BCE, in an environment where Aryan and indigenous South Asian cultures had been mingling for nearly a millennium. Thus, from the beginning this cultural environment contained some degree of common heritage with that of the Iranian plateau.

The Buddha's original teaching was more of a philosophy than a religion, though with the eventual popularization of his ideas came an ever-expanding array of religious beliefs and practices absorbed from the many local cultures where Buddhism took hold. The Buddha himself, whose given name was Siddhartha of the royal Gautama clan, developed a view of reality and a practice for living within that reality.[1] His teaching was summarized in Four Noble Truths: that life is suffering, that there is a cause of that suffering, namely desire, that there is a way to end suffering, and that the way is by following an Eightfold Path of right opinion, right thought, right speech, right activity, right livelihood, right effort, right attention, and right concentration.

Only later did many of the Buddha's followers popularize and fetishize what started out as simply a highly rigorous intellectual discipline. Since the first spread of Buddhism outside India was to the northwest among Iranian peoples, it was only natural that many of the local religious beliefs and practices of the latter would find their way into the popular Buddhist tradition.

Buddhism was the world's first universal philosophy. The Buddha taught that his analysis of the human predicament and the way out of it were not culture-bound, but true for everyone. Very soon Buddhist monks were setting out to spread the Buddha's teachings. There is even a legend that two Iranian merchants doing business in India, Tapassu, and Bhallika, heard the Buddha preach during his lifetime and brought his message back to their home province of Bactria. While there is no hard evidence of these two characters, their story is at least plausible. But it does not appear that Buddhism began to catch on widely until the reign of King Ashoka of the Maurya dynasty in the mid-third century BCE.

While some scholars now doubt whether Ashoka himself ever became a Buddhist, he at least supported the spread of Buddhist teaching, referred to simply as the *dharma*. Ashoka commissioned a number of Buddhist inscriptions on rocks and pillars throughout his realm, stretching across northern India to the eastern fringes of the Greek Seleucid empire which had replaced the Achaemenids only half a century earlier. At least six of Ashoka's inscriptions in northwestern India included translations into Aramaic, the language of the erstwhile Achaemenid bureaucracy and thus presumably aimed at Iranians. His royal edicts explicitly call for missionaries to spread the *dharma* to the Kambojas (Iranians) and the Yonas (Greeks). The Aramaic translations of Ashoka's edicts show some conscious attempt to add an Iranian flavor, such as frequent insertions of the qualifier "good" (a likely reference to "the good religion" of the Zoroastrians) and the deletion of references to *devas*, considered minor deities by Indians but abhorred as devils in Zoroastrianism.

Monks who wished to follow Ashoka's directives and spread the Buddha's teaching tended to travel along major trade routes, for obvious reasons. The dangers of long journeys called for the safety of numbers, and anyone wanting to travel would have been foolish not to attach himself to a caravan. The expansion of Buddhism was therefore intimately connected with long-distance trade.

These monks would occasionally settle and establish monasteries at various points along the trade routes. Over time traveling businessmen began stopping in at the monasteries during the course of their journeys. The monasteries not only provided lodging for laypeople sympathetic to Buddhism, they were also a place where travelers could make offerings to the Buddha in the form of donations, which gave them hope of a safe journey and enriched the monasteries in the process. Before long some monasteries had become quite wealthy indeed, enabling them to purchase farmland and other kinds of property. The symbiosis of lay and monastic Buddhists thereby created a mutually reinforcing economic stimulus for the growth and spread of the Buddhist community. Exactly the same pattern is seen later on in the spread of Christianity, Manichaeism, and Islam.

This northwestern region of the Indian subcontinent – roughly what is now Pakistan – was the transition zone between Iran and the Indian world, just as Mesopotamia was between Iran and the Semitic sphere. In the wake of Alexander's conquest Greek culture was added to the mix. Later the region would succumb to successive waves of Iranian and Turkish Central Asians seeking to control the trade networks, thereby bringing yet more cultural elements into this cosmopolitan environment. Buddhism, strengthened by its involvement in the long-distance trading economy, became the major religion in the area and would remain so up to the Arab conquests in the seventh century CE. But as a developing worldview, Buddhism in northwestern India was subject to influences emanating from all the diverse peoples of the region.

## Buddhism in eastern Iran

After the fall of the Maurya dynasty in the early second century BCE the eastern Iran–northwestern India border zone became an often unstable playing field on which various groups competed for power. These were mainly the Parthians from northeastern Iran; the Sakas

(Scythians), an originally nomadic Iranian people from the Eurasian steppes; and the Kushans, who also spoke an Iranian language (Bactrian) but were originally from the eastern part of Inner Asia and may have been partially descended from the Indo-European-speaking Tokharians. Each of these groups practiced religious tolerance, facilitating the co-mingling of ideas and the blending of traditions.

Buddhism's flourishing and development was due mainly to the support of traveling merchants who would make donations to Buddhist monasteries, called *viharas*, and shrines, called *stupas*, which usually contained relics associated with the Buddha. The economic and religious significance of the stupas carried over into the Muslim period and continues to the present day in Afghanistan and Central Asia. Muslim shrines to Sufi saints, like the stupas before them, are sites for pilgrimage and the main centers of popular religion. A symbol of this continuity can be seen in the banners once flown by Iranian Buddhists from the tops of the stupas, and which continue to adorn the cupolas of Sufi shrines in the region today.

In the centuries before the Arab conquests Buddhism was spread throughout the eastern Iranian world. Buddhist sites have been found in Afghanistan, Turkmenistan, Uzbekistan, and Tajikistan, as well as within Iran itself. It has long been known that the region of Bactria – what is now the northern part of Afghanistan and which remains largely Persian-speaking – was an important Buddhist center in the pre-Islamic period. What is only recently emerging, mainly from archeological work in Turkmenistan, is the important role played by Parthians in transmitting Buddhism centuries earlier. Although Chinese sources mention a number of important Buddhist monks who came from Parthia, such as the second-century translator of Buddhist texts An Shigao, most Western Buddhologists have considered that Buddhism caught on in only a minor way in Parthia itself.

Archeological work during the Soviet period tells a different story, however. Both the volume and distinctiveness of Buddhist artifacts from Parthian sites suggests a strong Buddhist presence there during Parthian and Kushan times, from around the first century until the third century when Sasanian power brought an increased support for Zoroastrianism.

Mariko Namba Walter has supported the view of Soviet scholarship, pointing out that Western scholars have only recently become aware of the extent of Soviet-era finds.[2] She notes that the Museum of Turkmen history in Ashgabat is full of Buddhist objects excavated from the Marv region, a once important trading center along the Silk Road until its destruction by the Mongols in the thirteenth century. Some one hundred Buddhist rock inscriptions – mainly dedications – have been found in Margiana, dating from the first century BCE through the fifth century CE. Sanskrit texts of the Sarvastivadin school, dating to the fifth century, have also been discovered there. Unfortunately, because scholarly work in Turkmenistan has slowed dramatically since the country's independence in 1991, most of this material remains unstudied and its significance poorly understood.

Western scholars have tended to see Buddhism as having been transmitted from Gandhara (northwestern India) directly to China via cities such as Khotan and Kucha in the Tarim Basin. Although one vector of transmission appears indeed to have gone this way over the rigorous passes of the Karakorum mountains, there is evidence of a western "detour" through Parthia as well. Though there are no surviving Buddhist texts in Parthian, the evolution of Buddhist terms in other languages suggests that at least in some cases, Buddhism was transmitted to China via Parthia. This would help explain why so many important Buddhist translators in China were of Parthian origin.

If Buddhism was prevalent in Parthia, which was centered in the northeastern part of the Iranian world, it is not clear how far its influence penetrated into the areas further west. Echoes of Buddhist ideas have been seen in some aspects of Christianity, and though the evidence for this is still rather foggy it is a fact that India and the Mediterranean were culturally connected (mainly through trade), and that this connection passed through Iran. Since Buddhism was strongly associated with trading activity, communities of Buddhist merchants from India lived in or traveled through western Iran. It is not known how successful the expatriate Indians were in winning converts to Buddhism in western Iran and Mesopotamia, but it would seem that the numbers of Buddhists in the west were far less than in the east.

The evidence for Buddhists in western Iran is limited. The Sasanian priest Kerdir mentions *sramana*s (Buddhist monks) among those non-Zoroastrians he hopes to eliminate. There are elements of Buddhist iconography in some Sasanian-period art. At Taq-e Bostan, for example, Mithra is seen standing on a lotus. Buddhist rock-cut monuments have been identified in the southern Iranian province of Fars, and recently nineteen Buddha statues, in the Gandhara style, were discovered there.[3] Place names give a further clue. A number of villages in western Khorasan – and even as far west as Rayy near modern Tehran – bear the name No Bahar, which is derived from Sanskrit *nava vihara* or "new [Buddhist] monastery."[4] Along the southern Iranian coast as well, the names Chah Bahar in Baluchistan and Botkhaneh ["Buddha-house"] and Baharistan in Fars attest to the passage of Buddhist traders from India. Tiz, on the Baluch coast near the border of Pakistan, is mentioned in the *Chach-nameh* as having had a substantial Buddhist community as late as the twelfth century, and may even have had a Buddhist administration in early Islamic times.

These are small signs, of course. On the other hand, while the importance of Buddhism in Parthia continues to be debated, the evidence from Bactria is very rich. One of the most striking examples of Iranian-Buddhist syncretism is an image of the Buddha found in Qara Tepe which bears the inscription "Buddha Mazda." This Kushan-period wall painting shows the Buddha surrounded by flames, apparently an evocation of Ahura Mazda himself.

The archeological remains of Buddhist stupas and monasteries throughout Bactria are supplemented by the many descriptions of Iranian Buddhist sites in the accounts of Buddhist travelers from China and elsewhere. The most famous of these is undoubtedly Xuanzang, a Chinese Buddhist monk who traveled via Central Asia to India in the early seventh century in hopes of finding authentic Sanskrit texts and bringing them back to China. Xuanzang states that in his time Balkh had about one hundred Buddhist monasteries and some three thousand monks, all belonging to schools of the "Lesser Vehicle" (Hinayana). His account takes note of the economic importance of these monasteries, which were often raided by nomadic armies:

> Outside the city, towards the southwest, there is a monastery called Navasangharama, which was built by a former king of this country. The Masters, who dwell to the north of the great Snowy Mountains, and are authors of the Shastras, occupy this monastery only, and continue their estimable labors in it. There is a figure of the Buddha here, which is lustrous with

noted gems, and the hall in which it stands is also adorned with precious substances of rare value. This is the reason why it has often been robbed by chieftains of neighboring countries, covetous of gain.

This monastery also contains a statue of Vaishravana Deva, by whose spiritual influence, in unexpected ways, there is protection afforded to the precincts of the monastery. Lately the son of Yeh-hu Khan, belonging to the Turks, becoming rebellious, Yeh-hu Khan broke up his camping ground, and marched at the head of the horde to make a foray against this monastery, desiring to obtain the jewels and precious things with which it was enriched. Having encamped his army in the open ground, not far from the monastery, in the night he had a dream. He saw Vaishravana Deva, who addressed him thus: "What power do you possess that you dare to overthrow this monastery?" and then hurling his lance, he transfixed him with it. The Khan, affrighted, awoke, and his heart penetrated with sorrow, he told his dream to his followers, and then, to atone somewhat for his fault, he hastened to the monastery to ask permission to confess his crime to the monks, but before he received an answer he died.[5]

Xuanzang then goes on to elaborate on the valuable relics contained in the monastery, which were objects of veneration for local Buddhists:

Within the monastery, in the southern hall of the Buddha, there is the washing basin which Buddha used. It contains about a peck, and is of various colors, which dazzle the eyes. It is difficult to name the gold and stone of which it is made. Again, there is a tooth of Buddha about an inch long, and about eight or nine tenths of an inch in breadth. Its color is yellowish white; it is pure and shining. Again, there is the sweeping brush of Buddha, made of the kasha plant. It is about two feet long and about seven inches round. Its handle is ornamented with various gems. These three relics are presented with offerings on each of the six fast-days by the assembly of lay and monastic believers. Those who have the greatest faith in worship see the objects emitting a radiance of glory.[6]

Clearly the Buddhist community of Balkh was more taken with miracles and ritual than with the sort of individual mental discipline originally taught by the Buddha a millennium or more earlier, but this was surely not atypical. It is hardly surprising that, according to Xuanzang, the monks of Balkh were so irregular in their observance of the monastic code (*vinaya*) "that it is hard to tell saints from sinners."

The close ties between Buddhist monks and government officials is also attested in an inscription which adorned the entrance to the No Bahar shrine, no longer extant but reported by the tenth-century Muslim historian Mas'udi in his book *Golden Meadows*:

> The Buddha said, "The courts of princes require three qualities: intelligence, reliability, and wealth."

Beneath this inscription, according to Mas'udi, someone had written in Arabic:

> The Buddha lied. What any free man possessing one of these qualities must do is avoid the court at all costs.[7]

A memory of the fabulous riches and adornment associated with the Buddhist shrines and statues of eastern Iran is preserved in the tradition of Persian Muslim poetry, which first took shape in precisely that part of the Iranian world where Buddhism had prevailed until the coming of Islam. The idealized "beloved" about whom the poets write (conceived of not as a girl but as an adolescent boy) is often described as a "moon-faced idol" (*bot* – literally, a buddha), and sometimes in terms of other details such as having "a body of silver," recalling the fact that buddha statues were often covered in silver paint. According to A. S. Melikian-Chirvani, "the poetic archtype of the idol [in Persian poetry] responds trait for trait to the artistic archetype of the eastern Iranian buddha."[8] Likewise, the poetic expression *ey bot* ("oh, beauty!") is a secular survival of the sacred Buddhist invocation *aho Buddho*.[9]

## Iranian influences in Buddhism

The subtle infusion of Iranian ideas into the spreading Buddhist tradition is most apparent in the contexts of Central Asian Iranian peoples such as the Sogdians of Transoxiana and the Sakas of Khotan. For example, Khotanese translations of *dharma* used the Iranian term *data* when referring to the Buddha's law. The term *Buddha-datu,* or "Buddha-law," may be compared with the earlier Zoroastrian *mazdo-data* (Mazda's law). Khotanese texts likewise employ the Iranian notion of *khvarna/farr* (Khotanese *pharra*) to mean "good fortune resulting from following the Buddha's path." Gandharan Buddhist art from the Kushan period occasionally employs the *khvarna* symbolism of flames rising from the Buddha's shoulders or encircling his head.

As in the Aramaic Ashokan inscriptions, Khotanese and Sogdian Buddhist writers avoided the term *deva.* In Khotan the Indian goddess of prosperity was replaced by her Iranian equivalent Shandramata (Spenta Armaiti). Mithra appears in Sogdian Buddhist texts and as a statue accompanying the smaller of the two colossal Buddhas at Bamiyan. Zurvan, the Iranian god of time, replaces Brahman in a Sogdian *jataka* (a story about the Buddha in his prior incarnations), while in some texts the Indian god Indra becomes Ohrmazd. The Buddhists were not entirely accommodating to Zoroastrianism, however. They were deeply critical of a number of Zoroastrian practices, including consanguineous marriage, the habitual killing of "evil" animals such as snakes and scorpions, and the exposing of corpses.

The square form of stupa-building was adopted by the Buddhists of eastern Iran from the region's pre-existing tradition of sacred archi-tecture, eventually becoming the norm throughout the Buddhist world. Another Iranian contribution to Buddhist architecture was the carving out of sacred grottos from rock – a technique inherited from Achaemenid funerary architecture – which spread to Buddhist sites throughout India and China. The most famous Iranian examples are the two colossal rock-cut buddha statues of the Bamiyan valley in Afghanistan, one measuring one hundred feet in height and the other one hundred and fifty, which dated to the sixth century CE. The taller one, which was apparently painted red, is referred to in medieval Muslim sources as "the Red Buddha," and the shorter one as "the White Buddha," presumably painted white. The two colossi survived until recent times when they were tragically destroyed by the fanatical Taliban regime in 2001.

Iranian influences are also present in the Buddhist art of the so-called Gandhara school, which arose under the Kushans in the first and second centuries CE. Representations of the Buddha in statues and paintings appear from this time onwards and are generally considered to emerge from Western forms, especially Greek but to some extent Iranian as well.

One distinctive feature in Gandhara art is the new prevalence of *bodhisattva* figures. Bodhisattvas are individuals who willingly postpone their own liberation so that they may work to help others reach that goal, on the principle that "none are saved until all are saved." The bodhisattva ideal is associated with the emergence of Mahayana ("Great Vehicle") Buddhism, a movement which arose in northwestern India and began to challenge the established schools (*nikaya*s, called Hinayana or "Lesser Vehicle" by the Mahayanists) some time shortly before the Common Era. The Mahayanists are characterized mainly by their identification with certain texts, many of which were apparently composed in the multicultural Indian-Iranian border region.

Finding Iranian figures and notions in the Mahayana system therefore comes as little surprise. Probably the most obvious is the bodhisattva Maitreya, the Buddha who will come as a savior figure in the future – a clear parallel to the Zoroastrian Saoshyant. Maitreya is the most common bodhisattva figure occurring in Gandharan art. Another bodhisattva, Amitabha, the Buddha of Light, bears many features associated with Zurvan. A third, Avalokiteshvara, shares certain elements in common with Mitra. In Khotanese Buddhist mythology we find the figure of Kshitigarbha, non-existent elsewhere in the Buddhist world, who conducts souls across the very Zoroastrian-sounding "bridge of death."

Just as some elements of Buddhist iconography appear in western Iran, numerous Sasanian features are found in the Buddhist art of the Iranian East. One such image is that of the griffin; another is that of a duck holding a necklace. In a seventh-century statue at Bamiyan, Maitreya is depicted wearing a crown identical to that of the Sasanian ruler Khosrow II. Many Bamiyan buddhas also wear hair ribbons of the Sasanian style.

Beginning in the Kushan period, Central Asian Buddhists began to build stupas to house relics of the Buddha. The architecture of many of these shrines, which allowed for circumambulation by pilgrims, seems to have been borrowed from that of Zoroastrian fire temples. The practice of adorning the shrines with flower garlands, prevalent in Bactria, was apparently carried over from a ritual associated with the Iranian goddess Anahita.

The merchants and missionaries who carried Buddhism to Central Asia and China were mostly of Iranian background. Many were Parthians, while others were Sogdians from what is now Uzbekistan, or Sakas from Khotan in what is now western China. Merchants and other travelers tended to be multilingual, and as such they often applied their skills to translating texts. Many translations of Buddhist works from Indian languages into Chinese were done by translators with Iranian names.

From the T'ang period onwards one of the most popular forms of Buddhism in China was the so-called "Pure Land" school, which taught that in order to be saved one merely had to be pronouncing the Buddha's name at the moment of death. Amitabha, the Buddha of Light, would then transport the devotee to a Pure Land of bliss, called Sukhavati, located somewhere in the West. This markedly soteriological faith is at odds with the "do-it-yourself" approach of early *nikaya* Buddhism in India, and seems to owe far more to Iranian tradition.

In another example, an annual ritual widely practiced in T'ang China, in which the "hungry ghosts" of departed ancestors are fed, resembles the Iranian "all souls" festival of Fravardigan, from which it may be derived. This is the contention of Iwamoto Yutaka, who proposes that the Chinese name for the festival comes (via Sogdian) from the Iranian word for "soul" (*ravan*) and suggests that the salvation story associated with it – in which the virtuous monk Mu-lien willingly descends into Hell to save his sinful mother – is a form of the Greek myth of Dionysos and Semele which was transmitted by Iranians to China.[10]

## The disappearance of Iranian Buddhism

Buddhism's spread to the West during Sasanian times was impeded by the state-supported power of the Zoroastrian magi. Iranian Buddhism was strongest in the East, in what is now northern and eastern Afghanistan, far from the center of Sasanian control. In the seventh century these territories were conquered by the Muslim Arabs, whose interest in controlling trade routes put them in direct economic competition with Buddhist merchants and monasteries.

Hostile references in the Qur'an to the "idol-worshipping" Meccan Arabs of Muhammad's time were easily transformed into ideological weapons against the Buddhists, who, unlike Christians, Jews, and Zoroastrians, were not offered the protection accorded under Islamic law to "peoples of the Book." As the Muslims consolidated their power in eastern Iran, Buddhists were easy prey, and by the ninth century it would seem that most Iranian Buddhists had abandoned their religion in favor of Islam.

Yet, as is most often the case with religious conversions, Iranian Buddhists who joined the Islamic community brought a number of influences with them. The Barmak family (possibly from *baramika*, "Buddhist priest;" they are known in European literature as the Barmecides) who held the reins of power as ministers in the Islamic caliphate during the first half of the ninth century, had originally been in charge of Buddhist shrines in the city of Balkh. Richard Bulliet has suggested that this heritage both provided the Barmaks with a regional power base of former Buddhists and enabled the central government in Baghdad to exercise control over eastern Iran through the Barmaks' influence.

Among the Sufis, the well-known early saint Ibrahim ibn Adham (d. ca. 790), also from Balkh, came from a Buddhist background as well. One of the first of the so-called "intoxicated" (i.e., ecstatic) Sufis, Abu Yazid (Bayazid) of Bistam (d. 874) was originally a disciple of an Indian teacher from Sindh, still a heavily Buddhist area at that time. Certain Buddhist ideas are detectable in the mystical philosophy of these and other eastern Iranian Sufis.

The notion of *fana'*, for example – interpreted in Islamic terms as "annihilation in God" as the ultimate goal of the mystic – bears a strong resemblance to the Buddhist concept of nirvana. Like earlier movements such as Manichaeism, Mazdakism, and the Abu Muslimiyya (all discussed in the following chapters), certain later heterodox "Islamic" sects such as the nominally Twelver Shi'ite Ahl-e Haqq in western Iran retain a belief in reincarnation which presumably has Buddhist or at least South Asian origins.

Buddhism experienced a brief revival in Iran during the second half of the thirteenth century under the Mongol dynasty known as the Il-khans. The founder of this dynasty, Hülegü Khan (r. 1256–1284) and his successor Arghun Khan (r. 1284–1291) were nominal Buddhists. They favored foreign Buddhist merchants over local Muslim ones, and allowed for the building of Buddhist institutions and the transfer of assets (a nice way of saying "looting") from Muslims to Buddhists. Needless to say these practices aroused the resentment and hostility of Iran's Muslim majority. After the conversion of the Mongol ruler Ghazan Khan to Islam around the turn of the fourteenth century Buddhist activity in Iran was quickly extinguished, and the newly built Buddhist monasteries and stupas either destroyed or converted into mosques. Buddhism has been essentially absent from Iran ever since.

# 5

# CHRISTIANITY

Iran was the springboard from which Christianity spread throughout Asia. The first Christian missionaries who brought their faith to China in the seventh century were from Iran, and for the next hundred years, Chinese sources continued to refer to Christianity as "the Persian religion." The Christians of southern India, who traced the origin of their community to the Apostle Thomas, were connected to Iran via sea routes and remained under the authority of the Iranian Church based in Mesopotamia. The history of Christianity's first millennium is as rich in the East as it is in the Mediterranean region, but it is a history that is scarcely known today.

Given the central importance of Iran in eastern Christianity, why is Iran's role generally neglected? One reason is that in a broad sense, the Christian mission in Asia was not a lasting success, since the overwhelming majority of the continent's inhabitants today belong to other faiths. Because Christianity became the dominant religion in Europe and in the Western hemisphere, it is most often thought of as a Western religion. Yet there were many Christians in Asia long before the faith caught hold in Europe, and their contributions to the histories of Asian cultures are vitally important.

Another factor is that eastern Christianity differs in many points of doctrine and practice from that of the West. The major forms of Christianity in Iran, Nestorianism and Jacobism, were both deemed heretical by the leaders of the state-supported Roman church during the course of ecumenical councils in the fifth century. Ever since that time, Western Christians have written of their Asian counterparts as misguided inferiors. To an objective historian, "heresy" is not a value judgment but merely describes a minority opinion. Unfortunately, an objective history of Asian Christianity has been very long in coming.

## The establishment of an Iranian church

Christian tradition has three "wise men" – identified in the Gospel of Matthew as Zoroastrian magi – following a star to the baby Jesus' manger in Bethlehem. Even leaving this story aside, Iran was surely one of the earliest places to hear the Christian gospel. The Book of the Acts of the Apostles (2:9) lists Jews from various regions of Iran among the witnesses to the miracle of the Pentecost, and it can be guessed that they did not hesitate to tell of this experience once they returned home.

For the first three centuries after the life of Jesus of Nazareth, Christians in Iran could practice and preach their faith far more easily than could their counterparts in the Roman world. In the Roman Empire Christians were seen as deviants from Judaism, lacking official status and legal protection. The persecutions of early Christians throughout the Mediterranean basin are well known.

Iran, meanwhile, was under the rule of the Parthians, whose religious policy was one of tolerance. Not until after the elevation of Zoroastrianism by the Sasanian government in the late third century would Christianity be treated in Iran as a suspect faith. But even the Sasanians recognized Christianity as a legitimate religion well before Emperor Constantine legalized it in the Roman Empire in 313 CE.

The favorable circumstances of Parthian rule allowed Christianity to spread and grow throughout Iran, apparently from missionary bases in northern Mesopotamia (Arbela and Edessa, modern Irbil in northern Iraq and Urfa in southeastern Turkey). There was a Christian bishop at Arbela by the year 104, and Christians are attested as far east as Bactria by 170. Christian refugees from the Roman Empire swelled the ranks of Iranian converts; by the year 225 twenty bishoprics had been established throughout the Parthian-held lands. A group of sixty Christian tombs on the small island of Kharg in the Persian Gulf has been dated to 250, and a Christian church has been excavated there as well.[1] Resettlements of civilians following Sasanian victories over the Romans in 256 and 260 brought both Greek- and Syriac-speaking Christians to live in Iranian territories. (Syriac is a Semitic language, a dialect of Aramaic.)

By the late third century Christians in Iran were so numerous that the zealot Zoroastrian priest Kerdir, seeking to eradicate competing religions from the realm, felt threatened enough to call for their elimination. Even so, conversions to Christianity appear to have continued steadily over the following centuries. In 562, King Khosrow I decreed that any proselytization by Christians in Iran would be punishable by death.

With the rise in status of Christianity to state religion of the Roman Empire in the fourth century and military setbacks inflicted by Rome on the Sasanians, Iranian Christians were saddled with the additional suspicion of belonging to the faith of the enemy. This was especially the case from 340 to 379, during the latter part of the reign of Shapur II, when they were severely persecuted. Regularly denounced by Mazdaean priests as a potential fifth column for the Romans, Iranian Christians were arrested in great numbers and subjected to all manner of tortures to force them to apostasize. A royal decree enumerates the "crimes" of which they were accused:

> The Christians destroy our holy [Zoroastrian] teaching, and teach men to serve one God, and not to honor the Sun, or Fire. They defile Water by their ablutions, they refrain from marriage and the propagation of children, and refuse to go to war with the King of Kings. They have no rules about the slaughter and eating of animals; they bury the corpses of men in the earth. They attribute the origin of snakes and creeping things to a good God. They despise many servants of the King, and teach witchcraft.[2]

Even more significantly, perhaps, the Christians refused Shapur's demand that they pay double taxes!

After Shapur's death in 379, however, the persecution of Christians abated and doctrinal disputes within the Roman church caused many followers of non-authorized Christian sects to seek refuge in Iran. One of the thorniest disagreements in the early church was over the nature of Christ. Some held that in Jesus both a divine nature and a human one were fused. This was the monophysite position, whose adherents came to be known as Jacobites after bishop Jacob bar Addai who was one of its later proponents. Others believed that these natures remained separate and that two distinct persons, one human and one divine, inhabited the historical Jesus. This so-called "diophysite" view was associated with the bishop of Constantinople, Nestorius of Antioch, and its followers were called Nestorians. The monophysite dogma prevailed at the Council of Ephesus in 431, but at the Council of Chalcedon in 451 both positions were rejected in favor of a compromise belief, "one person, two natures," which became the orthodoxy of the Byzantine church.

Reduced to the status of heretics in the Roman world, monophysites and diophysites alike found greater freedom in Iran. The Iranian church broke away definitively from Byzantium following the Council of Ephesus, establishing its new seat at the Sasanian capital of Ctesiphon in Babylonia under the leadership of an autonomous Patriarch, whom they called the Catholicos. This break represented a rejection of Byzantine religious authority, but also of its political authority over Iranian Christians. An Iranian synod held in 486 rejected the asceticism and monasticism which were central to Byzantine Christianity, abolishing the practice of celibacy, and made diophysitism the official doctrine of the Iranian church. The theology and ascetic tendencies of the monophysites were marginalized, but did not disappear from Iran. Armenia, which was under Sasanian rule much of the time, became officially Christian in the early fourth century, around the time that Christianity was recognized in the Roman Empire.[3] Following the Arab conquests in the mid-seventh century groups of Jacobites were deported from Edessa to Herat and elsewhere in eastern Iran, where they became numerous enough to establish two bishoprics.

The treatment of Christians by the Sasanian state varied greatly depending on changing circumstances. They were tolerated by most Sasanian governments, but there were three periods of major persecutions. During the reign of Shapur II an estimated 35,000 Christians were killed. A second wave, instigated by the prime minister Mihr Narseh, took place during the 420s under Bahram V. The persecutions of Yazdigerd II (r. 439–457) took the highest toll, resulting in the deaths of as many as 150,000 Christians. In many cases Iranian Christians seem to have sought out their martyrdom, deliberately provoking Zoroastrians by putting out or defiling their sacred fires and committing other acts of sacrilege. But even at the worst of times Christianity was never actually a banned religion in Iran, as it had been in the Roman Empire for three centuries.

Though sporadic persecutions of Christians occurred throughout the Sasanian period, certain rulers were more sympathetic. Yazdigerd I (r. 399–421) was hailed in Christian documents as "the victorious and glorious king" – some even claimed that he was a Christian. (Zoroastrian texts, by contrast, refer to him as *winahgar*, "the sinner.") Khosrow II (r. 591–628) had two influential Christian wives and a Christian court physician. The last Sasanian emperor, Yazdigerd III, fleeing the Arab armies in the mid-seventh century, is said to have had a Christian burial following his death at Marv in eastern Iran in 651.

It has been suggested that by the late Sasanian period Christianity had become the most powerful challenge to state Zoroastrianism, even that it was on the verge of becoming Iran's majority religion. This hypothesis is impossible to substantiate, but there is evidence that Christians were numerous enough that the state required their support. In the late sixth century the emperor Hormizd IV (r. 579–590) wrote a letter to his priests instructing them to end their persecutions of Christians and others, whom he refers to as the "hind legs" of the Empire:

> Even as our royal throne cannot stand upon its two front legs without the back ones, so also our government cannot stand and be secure, if we incense the Christians and the adherents of other religions, who are not of our faith. Cease therefore to harass the Christians, but exert yourselves diligently in doing good works, so that the Christians and the adherents of other religions, seeing that, may praise you for it and feel themselves drawn to our religion.[4]

Whatever the actual numbers of Christians in Iran, their importance was disproportionately high especially in the realm of higher learning. Like the Jews, Christians with their cosmopolitan influences and knowledge of languages were in a position to act as transmitters of culture across and beyond the Iranian world. Having access to the wisdom of ancient Greece, they often served as physicians. As the "pagan" knowledge of the Classical Mediterranean became increasingly rejected in the now Christian West, those who possessed such knowledge found refuge in Iran. The Nestorians were ejected from their academy at Edessa after Nestorius was anathematized by the Council of Ephesus in 431. At first many relocated further east to Nisibis in Sasanian Mesopotamia. Eventually the center of Nestorian learning became their medical school at Gondeshapur in the southwestern Iranian province of Khuzestan. The Gondeshapur academy was under the directorship of the Christian Bokhtishu family, who provided several generations of physicians to the Sasanian royal court. The school survived into Islamic times, when Christian teachers trained the sons of many families from among the Arab elite.

It was mainly the Iranian Nestorians who brought Christianity to Central Asia and China via the Silk Roads, although Jacobite and Melkite (Byzantine) communities were also present. Iranian missionaries, working in tandem with (or at times identical to) traveling merchants, made contact with the nomadic Turkic-speaking peoples of Inner Asia by the sixth century, apparently using their charisma and perhaps magic to persuade them to accept Christian priests as substitutes for their traditional shamans. One story has a Christian missionary stopping a thunderstorm where local shamans had been unable to do so.

The Nestorian Patriarch of Baghdad Timothy I (780–823) expanded the missionary effort to Central Asia, which in his time lay at the fringes of Muslim power. The so-called Nestorian monument at Xian, which tells the early history of Christians in China, was erected in 781 under the direction of an Iranian named Yazdbozed. The Iranian church also had ties to Christian communities in southern India, where a number of documents and inscriptions in the Middle Persian language (Pahlavi) attest to the presence of Iranians, presumably merchants.

The liturgical languages of Iranian Christians were Syriac and, in Central Asia, Sogdian, an Iranian dialect formerly spoken in what is now Uzbekistan and which was the lingua franca of the Silk Roads in pre-Islamic times. (A modern variant of Sogdian is still spoken in the Yaghnob valley of Tajikistan.) Syriac and Sogdian Christian texts and loanwords are found in China from the seventh century onwards, and in western Tibet two centuries later. Excavations in the early twentieth century in western China uncovered a tenth-century

Christian monastery containing a library with many texts in Syriac and Sogdian. Slightly later Christian texts from nearby sites are in Turkic. Christianity continued to exist among the Iranian and Turkic-speaking peoples of Central Asia well into the fourteenth century, when it was extinguished by the fanatical Tamerlane.

## *Iranian Christian polemics against other religions*

Christian writings in Syriac from the Sasanian period reflect themes consistent with the view of an embattled minority. In the fourth century, at the time of Shapur II's persecutions, there is a flourishing of martyr literature. There are polemics against the Zoroastrian reverence for the sun, fire, and water as representing worship of Creation instead of the Creator. To a Christian this could indeed appear to be the case, although as described earlier, the traditional Iranian view (that is, of *mainyu*s) did not make such a radical disjunction between a deity and the substance associated with it, the doctrine of God's absolute transcendence being a more recent innovation.

Christian writers mock the "mumbling" recitations of the Zoroastrian magi, who perhaps understood little of their own formulas. By contrast, Christian priests and monks of the period are often characterized by their literacy, which was based on reading the Bible. Christian texts also criticize the Zoroastrian preference for marriage among close relatives. In return, contemporary Zoroastrian works, including the *Denkard* (the "Acts of Faith") and the *Shkandgumanig wizar* (the "Doubt-Destroying Exposition"), accused Christians of depopulating the world through the practice of celibacy, and ridiculed them for claiming that a good God could create evil things (such as snakes), that he was born of a woman, and that the Supreme Being could have been crucified and killed. Despite these ongoing exchanges, however, it has been noted that in Sasanian times Christians and Jews devoted more energy to refuting each other than they did to criticizing Zoroastrians.[5]

One of the most vociferous defenders of Iranian Christianity was the fourth-century monk Aphrahat of Mar Mattai (near Nineveh), a convert from Zoroastrianism whom Jacob Neusner has called "the first Iranian church father." Aphrahat wrote long polemics against Iranian Jews, whom he saw as having irredeemably relinquished their status as chosen people to the Christians. Though there is nothing unique in this position, what is distinctive about Aphrahat's argument is his insistence that the Jews' observation of God's commandments had *never* brought them salvation, even in pre-Christian times.

Aphrahat was disturbed by what he perceived to be an undue concern by Iranian Christians with the beliefs and practices of their "misguided" Jewish neighbors. This explains his deep obsession with distinguishing the Christian Easter celebration from the Jewish Passover in the following passage:

> You have heard, my beloved, concerning this paschal sacrifice, that I said to you that it was given as a mystery to the prior people [i.e., the Jews], and its truth today is known among the peoples. Greatly troubled are the minds of foolish and unintelligent folk concerning this great day of festival, as to how they should understand and observe it . . .
>
> The paschal sacrifice of the Jews is the day of the fourteenth [of Nisan], night and day. But for us the day of the great passion is Friday, the fifteenth, night and day. Then after the paschal sacrifice Israel eats unleavened bread seven days until the twenty-first of the month. But we observe as the festival of unleavened bread the festival of our redeemer. They eat unleavened bread with bitter herb. But our redeemer rejected that cup of bitterness and removed all bitterness from the peoples when he tasted but did not wish to drink. The Jews recall concerning themselves their own sins from festal to festal season, but we recall the crucifixion and the pain of our redeemer.
>
> They on the paschal sacrifice went forth from the slavery of the Pharaoh, but we on the day of His crucifixion were redeemed from the slavery of Satan. They sacrificed a lamb from the flock, and with its blood they were saved from the destroyer, but we through the blood of the Chosen Son were redeemed from the works of destruction which we were doing . . .
>
> Now be persuaded by this small essay which I have written to you, for you are *not* commanded to be vexed with word-games, matters in which there is no profit, but [to preserve] a pure heart which keeps the commandment and the festival and the times of the observances of each day.[6]

It would seem from this and other examples that in the mixed cultural environment of northern Mesopotamia, the lines between religious communities in the Sasanian period were not so clearly drawn. A church synod in 585 drew attention to this fact:

> We have learned that some Christians, either through ignorance or through imprudence, are going to see people of other religions and taking part in their feasts, that is to say, going to celebrate feasts with Jews, heretics [i.e., non-Nestorian Christians] or pagans [Zoroastrians], or even accepting something sent to them from the feasts of other religions. We thus prescribe, by heavenly authority, that a Christian must not go to the feasts of those who are not Christians, nor accept anything sent to Christians from those feasts, for it is part of the oblation made in their sacrifice.[7]

More serious still, perhaps, was the threat of eroding communal boundaries through sexual relationships and marriage, a concern shared by Christian, Zoroastrian, and Jewish leaders alike. A seventh-century church text shows the extent of the priests' fears:

> Women who have a faith believing in Christ and who wish to live the Christian life must guard themselves with all their might against union with pagans [i.e., Zoroastrians], seeing that the union with them creates for them usages contrary to the fear of God and drags their will into laxity. So Christians should absolutely avoid living with pagans; and he who would dare to do so would be expelled from the church and from all Christian honor, by the word of Our Lord.[8]

It may be noted that the preoccupation of church leaders with what might seem minor details (such as the disagreements over dates or the sharing of meals with unbelievers), as well as with the prevention of miscegenation, is typical of priestly types in all religions, who more than any other social group are concerned with creating and maintaining distinctions between "us" and "them." Laypeople, by and large, are less concerned under normal circumstances with the blurring of boundaries, although in times of social stress, when scapegoats are needed, such differences are more readily perceived and acted upon.

Sacred art is another domain in which such boundary-crossing frequently occurs. Notwithstanding their ideological hostility to other faiths, Christians in the Sasanian world were not above appropriating certain aspects of Zoroastrian iconography. The old Iranian symbol for glory (*farr*) was often expressed in Sasanian times by framing an image in a ribbon with its loose ends fluttering upwards. In Christian Georgia, which was a Sasanian province, a sixth-century church has a cross framed in this manner. Georgian coins of the same period were struck in imitation of Sasanian ones, with the exception that they replaced the image of a fire on the Sasanian coins with one of a cross. Iranian Christian seals from the period often bear Sasanian symbols such as the winged lion (associated with St. Mark).

Another documented Iranian Christian apologist of the Sasanian period is Mihram Gushnasp (d. 614), a convert from Zoroastrianism who served at the royal court. The *Acts of the Persian Martyrs* records the following dialogue between Mihram (also known by his Christian title of St. George) and a Zoroastrian priest:

Priest: We in no way hold fire to be God, but only pray to God through fire, as you do through the Cross.

Mihram: But we do not say, as you do to the fire, "We pray to you, Cross, God."

Priest: That is not so.

Mihram: So you have it in your Avesta that it *is* a god.

Priest: We reverence fire because it is of the same nature as Ormazd.

Mihram: Does Ormazd have everything which fire has?

Priest: Yes.

Mihram: Fire consumes dung and horse-droppings, and, in brief, whatever comes to it. Since Ormazd is of the same nature, does he also consume everything like it?[9]

As the source in question is a Christian text, the priest's reply to this challenge, if he offered one, is not recorded.

Mihram's sister, whom, following Zoroastrian tradition, he had married, proved an even more zealous convert to Christianity. Following her miraculous cure from a severe illness, she demonstrated her rejection of Zoroastrianism by defiling a sacred fire, handling it while in an impure state of menstruation, casting it to the ground, and stamping it out with her feet. It would be hard to imagine a way of combining insults that would be more horrifying to the Zoroastrian priests of the court.

## *Iranian Christians under Muslim rule*

By the early seventh century it would appear that western Iran, particularly the Mesopotamian provinces, was largely Christian. Most of the Christian population was of Aramaic-speaking Semitic stock, but as indicated above, their attempts to convert ethnic Iranians were often successful. The Arab conquests, however, put an end to the expansion of Christianity in Iran. Like the Zoroastrians and the Jews (but not the Buddhists or Manichaeans), under Islamic law Christians constituted a recognized religious community (*dhimmi*), a "people of the Book" (*ahl al-kitab*) granted the protection of the Muslim state in return for payment of a special tax, the *jizya*. (The *jizya* was a survival of a similar Sasanian tax known as the *gazidag*.)

But as a religious minority the Christians were also subject to restrictions and discrimination, and were often singled out as scapegoats in times of social unrest. They were not supposed to build any new churches, on the assumption that while they were free to follow an obsolete religion if they chose, rational people would inevitably come to see that Islam was a superior religion so it was inconceivable (from the Muslim point of view) that the numbers of Christians would grow – hence no need for more churches. They were also not supposed to erect any structures taller than those built by Muslims. They should not ring church bells, and they were forbidden from drinking alcohol in public or allowing their pigs to be seen by Muslims. They were not to ride horses (though donkeys and mules were permitted), and they should wear a distinctive mark and belt. They could not insult Islam or its prophet, proselytize to Muslims, or marry Muslim women. Muslim men, however, could marry non-Muslim women, on the somewhat dubious premise that the children of a Muslim father would thereby receive a proper Muslim upbringing.

Thus, though in many ways Arab rule was an improvement over that of the Sasanians, Christians and Jews lived amidst a plethora of reminders that they were still second-class citizens. Christian sources of the seventh century are heavy with themes of apocalypse and retribution. Many saw the Muslim conquests as a form of divine reckoning against the corrupt Zoroastrians, while others interpreted them as punishment for the Christians' own laxity, for example, embracing the "heresy" of monophysitism or converting to Islam. The Persian monk John of Phenek wrote of the Arabs in the 690s:

> We should not think of their advent as something ordinary, but as due to divine working. Before calling them, God had prepared them beforehand to hold Christians in honor; thus they had a special commandment from God concerning our monastic station, that they should hold it in honor ... How otherwise, apart from God's help, could naked men, riding without armor or shield, have been able to win; God called them from the ends of the earth in order to destroy, through them, a sinful kingdom (Amos 9:8), and to humiliate, through them, the proud spirit of the Persians.[10]

Like the Jews the Christians were left to run their own internal affairs in their own way and were represented by the recognized head of their community, the *Resh galuta* or Exilarch in the case of the Jews and the Nestorian Catholicos in the case of the Iranian Christians. This set a longstanding precedent whereby various non-Muslim communities under Muslim rule would be treated as a "nationality" (*millet*) under the direct jurisdiction of their own religious leader who was answerable on their behalf to the Muslim authorities. The Christian hierarchy in Iran thus became responsible not only for tax collection but also the range of internal legal matters and social organization within the Christian community – a kind of state-within-a-state. Only when conflicts transgressed community boundaries were the Muslim authorities supposed to become involved.

The Arabs, who lacked prior experience in administering an empire, employed many Christians to serve in their bureaucracy. They also gave their support to the Christian academies of Nisibis, Gondeshapur, and Marv, which continued to provide trained civil servants and also began accepting Muslim students. Christians and Jews were favored as court physicians, secretaries, and astronomers. When the capital of the Caliphate was moved from Syria to Mesopotamia following the Iranian-led Abbasid revolution in 750, Iranian Christians began to play an even more central role in government. The Nestorian Patriarch Timothy I in particular was very close with the Abbasid Caliph al-Mahdi, and together the two sponsored a number of inter-religious dialogues between scholars. One thing they could agree upon was their dislike of the Jews.

In the early ninth century the Caliph Ma'mun founded an institute at Baghdad called the *Bayt al-hikma* (the "House of Wisdom") and appointed a Nestorian, Hunayn ibn Ishaq, to head it. Hunayn himself translated over one hundred books from Greek and Syriac into Arabic, and presided over the translation of many others. Christians thus played a major role in transmitting Greek knowledge to the Muslim world, just as Spanish Jews would do in passing that knowledge back to Europe several centuries later.

Over time the influence of prominent Christians within the Caliphate led to a degree of Muslim resentment, and in the ninth century increased efforts were made to "Islamicize" the administration. Many Christians and others maintained their positions by embracing Islam. The Crusades, though they did not affect Iran directly, were an additional cause of resentment towards Christians among Iranian Muslims.

Christians in Iran experienced a brief improvement in status following the Mongol conquests in the thirteenth century. The Mongols had an opportunistic approach to religion – whatever seemed to work, they would approve and try to use for their benefit. They were, accordingly, reluctant to privilege any one religion for fear of losing access to others.

Under Mongol rule certain factors did work to the advantage of Christians, however. Most of the rulers who had resisted the Mongol armies had been Muslims. This, combined with the fact that Muslims controlled the long-distance trade across much of Asia, left a residue of distrust on the part of the Mongols. Also, within the ruling Mongol family a number of important women had learned Christianity from Nestorian missionaries. Finally, the Mongols had hopes of establishing alliances with Christian Europe against the Muslim states of the Near East. After the Mongol army sacked Baghdad and killed the Caliph in 1258, those of Iran's Christians who were fortunate enough to survive the initial slaughter found they often had a sympathetic ear at the Mongol court.

Muslims, for their part, found the Mongols barbaric and were initially reluctant to serve them. As a result, Christians were once again able to find important posts in the new government bureaucracy, especially once the Mongols in Iran (the Il-khans) set up their capital at Tabriz in heavily Christian Azerbaijan. The second Il-khan ruler, Abaqa (d. 1282), actually decreed that government clerks had to be either Christian or Jewish. Unfortunately many Iranian Christians were less than gracious in taking advantage of their improved status, using it to settle scores with Muslim rivals and offending them by drinking and carousing in public. In Baghdad the Patriarch Mar Denha I had a number of formerly Christian Muslims drowned in the Tigris River. During this time Roman Catholic monks from Europe arrived in Iran and set up missions throughout the northwestern part of the country.

The Christians' newfound strength was short-lived, however. The Il-khans eventually saw fit to align themselves with Iran's Muslim majority, and after his accession in 1304 Ghazan Khan embraced Islam. No longer protected by the favor of their Mongol overlords, Iranian Christians were devastated by Muslim pogroms during the first decades of the fourteenth century. The Central Asian Turk Tamerlane, who saw himself both as a second Chinggis Khan and as a restorer of mainstream Sunni ("traditionalist") Islam against Shi'ites and other "heretics," delivered the *coup de grâce* when he conquered Iran in 1394, destroying churches and monasteries and massacring Christians as he went.

Though Christian communities survived in Iran, after the tribulations of the fourteenth century their numbers became greatly reduced – mainly, one may suppose, through conversion to Islam – and largely restricted to the region of Lake Urmia in the northwestern part of the country. As a result of Catholic missionary efforts in the mid-seventeenth century some of the Nestorian Christians in western Iran and northern Mesopotamia accepted the authority of the Pope in Rome; from 1844 these Uniates were formally designated by the Ottoman government as "Chaldeans," a title that the Nestorians (who most often referred to themselves simply as "Syrians") had occasionally claimed as well.

## Armenian Christians in Iran

The Indo-European-speaking people of Armenia, a land stretching southwards from the Caucasus mountains, have a long history of interaction with their Iranian neighbors. Armenia was under the rule of Iranian dynasties for much of its history, beginning with the Achaemenids in the sixth century BCE when the province is first mentioned. The pagan beliefs and practices of pre-Christian Armenia were heavily infused with borrowings from ancient Iranian religion, though the Armenians apparently did not possess the Avesta. Their chief deity was Aramazd – that is, Ahura Mazda. The goddess Anahita and the god Mithra were also highly revered.

Following their adoption of Christianity as state religion in the early fourth century, Armenians became a major Christian presence on the northwestern fringes of the Iranian world. Armenian Christianity preserves many ancient Iranian features, however, even to the present day. For example, on the eve of the Christian Ascension, Armenians go out to collect flowers they call *hawrot-mawrot*, which are named for the Amesha Spentas of health and immortality, Haurvatat and Ameretat. The Armenian cross has a solar symbol at its center and rests upon a bed of flames. Small numbers of Armenians never converted to Christianity but continued to practice Zoroastrianism up to the twentieth century.

Throughout the Muslim period Armenia was an oft fought-over middle zone, occasionally independent but mostly under the rule of various Muslim dynasties. Armenians frequently served as the go-betweens among the rival powers of Christian Europe, the Muslim world, and even China and India.

By the early seventeenth century the Armenian lands were being devastated by endless battles between the empires of Safavid Iran and Ottoman Turkey. In 1605 the Safavid king Abbas I, as part of a scorched-earth policy aimed at the Ottomans, uprooted over 300,000 Armenians from the region of Jolfa on the Araxes River and resettled them in his capital of Esfahan in central Iran.[11] Armenians became the leading craftsmen, bankers, and businessmen of the city, and played a major role in Iran's silk trade. In 1638 an Armenian of Esfahan published the first-ever printed book in the Middle East.

Armenians have been the most numerous and significant Christian minority in Iran since their forced transplantation in the seventeenth century. New Jolfa, on the southern bank of the Zayandeh River, remains a visibly Armenian enclave, though Armenians now live all throughout the country. Most Armenians in Iran belong to the Armenian Apostolic (monophysite) Church, although there are small numbers of Armenian Catholics and Protestants as well.

## European Christian missions

After a three-hundred-year hiatus, Roman Catholic emissaries were sent to Iran from the early seventeenth century as European states sought alliances against the Ottomans. Shah Abbas I granted certain concessions to European Christians who came to live or do business in Iran, although they were not allowed to proselytize among Muslims. According to Islamic law apostasy is a capital offense, reflecting the Islamic notion that while Judaism and Christianity are legitimate revealed religions, Islam supersedes them and having understood this a Muslim could not conceivably "go back."

When France, England, and the United States began sending missionaries to Iran in the early nineteenth century, this policy continued. As a result, European missionaries competed with each other to "convert" Iranian Christians to their own denominations. The French in particular took to opening schools, and increasing numbers of young Iranians learned French as their gateway to the world of European science and letters.

Efforts by Protestants from England and the United States were spurred by the translation of the Bible into modern Persian by the Englishman Henry Martyn in 1812. The first American missionaries, a Presbyterian minister named Justin Perkins and his wife, settled in the heavily Nestorian region of Urmia in Azerbaijan in 1834. The Perkinses somewhat misleadingly described the Nestorian communities to be living a generally comfortable life, free to remain home and tend their fields while their Muslim neighbors got conscripted for military service. (In fact they were mostly poor tenant farmers.) Although the Nestorians did not proselytize, sick Muslims often came to their churches seeking the prayers of the priests and hoping to be cured. These Muslims would frequently kiss the cross and the Bible and leave offerings to the Christian saints.

Over the next fifty years the American missions established eighty-one schools throughout Iran. The Presbyterians brought modern medicine to the country, setting up their first hospital in Urmia in 1882. Scholars have generally considered that it was the

Western missionaries who created the historical association, based mainly on geography, by which Iran's Nestorian Christians came to call themselves "Assyrians," a name by which they are known today (*Assuri* in Persian). Assyrians themselves, however, contest this interpretation, claiming much older roots for their present self-designation.

Apart from access to schools and hospitals, part of the appeal for Iranian Christians to embrace Western forms of Christianity was to secure the protection of Western governments. And indeed, throughout the nineteenth century American, British, and French officials frequently intervened with the Iranian authorities on behalf of their Iranian converts, for example in mitigating some of the customary legal discriminations to which Christians were subjected in Muslim society. One such case was in 1881 when the British ambassador was able to pressure the Iranian government to rewrite a number of laws, including the one which specified that if a Christian converted to Islam he would inherit the property of all his relatives. (The law nevertheless continued to be applied until the 1940s.)

Although the Presbyterian and Anglican missions were the most visible, by the end of the nineteenth century nine different Christian denominations were competing to convert the Iranian Christians. Throughout the country efforts were made to win over Jews and Zoroastrians as well. A number of Iranian Muslims also made use of the missionaries' medical and educational facilities, and despite the Islamic laws at least some Muslims converted to Christianity. Obviously all these developments, from the interference of foreign powers to the conversions of Muslims, aggravated relations between Iranian Christians and their Muslim neighbors on the local level.

In 1932 the Pahlavi government nationalized all elementary education, and two years later American missionaries were expelled from Urmia. Under the nationalist Mosaddeq regime in the early 1950s the activities of foreign missionaries were further curtailed. But by that time Iranian converts were numerous enough to maintain the work of the missions on their own, now using the Persian language rather than Aramaic. Christian missionary work was definitively halted, however, following the revolution of 1979.

# 6

# GNOSTIC TRADITIONS

The term "Gnosis" is used to describe an esoteric religiosity which began to emerge in the eastern Mediterranean region a little before the beginning of the Common Era. It was not a religion *per se*, but rather an *approach* to religion which could be expressed from within the matrices of diverse faith systems. The label itself derives from the Greek word "gnosis," which means "to know," in the sense of intuitive rather than cognitive knowledge. The basic notion is that salvation can be attained through acquiring the right kind of knowledge.

The Gnostic approach is characterized by a number of recurring themes and perceptions. One is a radically dualistic view of the universe, in which good is associated with spirit and evil with matter. Spirit is symbolized by light, and matter by darkness. Humans are seen as being in a wretchedly fallen state, entrapped in a repulsive and impure material existence. The Gnostic seeks to transcend this condition through various forms of self-purification, ultimately returning to his or her original, spiritual existence. It is generally understood that this salvation will be the privilege of only a select few who are able to apprehend deep truths beyond the ken of the many. The ritual of baptism is often central, representing one form of initiation into the Gnostics' esoteric world.

In the Gnostic worldview Greek, Semitic, and Iranian influences can all be detected. The spirit-matter dichotomy echoes Platonic thought, while the dualism of good and evil and its light-dark symbolism are drawn from Iranian religion. The practice of baptism and its associated notions of purification, renewal, and sublime insight is very old, being found among the ancient Egyptians, the Greeks, and others. Gnostic cosmologies, together with a strong interest in astronomy and numerology, show continuities from the knowledge systems of ancient Babylonia.

The origins of Gnosticism are hopelessly buried amidst the underground activities of a plethora of secretive sects from remote antiquity. By the beginning of the Common Era, however, specific Gnostic movements are known from the sources. Some of these arose from within Jewish society, others from among Christian or other groups, but in most cases such distinctions were clouded and Gnostics drew variously from the complete range of traditions existing at the time, giving each their own distinctive interpretation.

## Mandaeism

The Mandaeans (from the Aramaic *manda*, "to know") are the only surviving Gnostics in Iran, and they may have been the first. The sect traces its origins to a Jewish community originally from the Jordan valley prior to the time of Jesus. They revere John the Baptist as their prophet, considering Jesus to be merely one of John's wayward disciples. Like other unrecognized religious groups they suffered persecution both from the Roman provincial administrators and from the local Jewish authorities. As many others had done and would continue to do, they eventually chose exile under the more tolerant rule of the Parthians further east. Exactly when this took place is unclear, but it was probably sometime between the first and third centuries of the Common Era.

The particular history of the Mandaean community is difficult to follow – there were many diverse Gnostic-baptist sects in Mesopotamia during the Parthian period – but they may be connected with the pagan Sabeans of Harran mentioned in Muslim sources.[1] (The modern Persian term for the Mandaeans, *sobbi*, derives from the Arabic term for "baptizers.") Like the Mandaeans today, the Sabeans possessed a highly sophisticated cosmology and astronomical knowledge based on that of ancient Babylonia, which often earned them positions as advisors at court or teaching in academies.

The Mandaean sacred text, called the Ginza, was apparently compiled from oral tradition at the time of the Arab conquests. The Qur'an instructed the Arabs to accord protection to "peoples of the [sacred] book," and the Mandaeans were quick to prove that they possessed one. Nevertheless, in actual practice the Mandaeans would often suffer the same types of discrimination and occasional persecutions to which other "protected communities" were subjected under Muslim rule.

Typical of Gnostic traditions, Mandaeism sees humans as existing in a fallen state, striving to regain their true home in the heavenly "World of Light" above. This world and the World of Light are connected, principally through the activities of supernatural beings called *'utra*s ("angels" or "guardians") who remain in contact with Mandaeans. They are ruled over by a supreme deity referred to as the First Life. The universe also includes evil spirits associated with the planets and the zodiac, who are the children of the evil female spirit Ruha. Each human has a heavenly spirit twin. The aim of Mandaeans is to ascend to the World of Light and attain reunion with their spiritual counterparts. There is an underworld of darkness in opposition to the World of Light, but bad Mandaeans do not go there; rather, they experience a series of posthumous purifications so that they may ascend to the World of Light.

The central ritual for Mandaeans is baptism (*masbuta*) in flowing water, which is seen as a manifestation of the World of Light on earth. They are baptized not just once but numerous times throughout their lives. Mandaeans believe that when there are no more Mandaeans in the world, the world will come to an end.

## Manichaeism

Within the exceptionally rich hybrid religious atmosphere of third-century Mesopotamia arose what would for a thousand years be one of the major world religions, but which by the fortunes of history is no longer practiced by anyone in the world today. This was Manichaeism, perhaps the most maligned religion in history. For centuries it was known only through the polemics of its worst enemies, such as St. Augustine of Hippo in the Christian tradition and the various heresiographers and historians of Islam. Byzantine writers derisively termed it a *"mania,"* punning on the founder's name. Even Chinese sources dismissed Manichaeism as a sect of "vegetarian demon-worshippers."

Yet for all the venomous attacks of its adversaries, Manichaeism must be ranked as one of the most influential religions in history, if for no other reason than that its proselytizing successes and extreme doctrinal positions forced apologists for other faiths to refine and strengthen their own views. It was largely opposition to the exploding popularity of Manichaeism that energized the Zoroastrian magi to lobby so aggressively for their own religion's official status in the Sasanian Empire. St. Augustine was a Manichaean for ten years before converting to Christianity, and his understanding of the latter faith was greatly influenced by his rejection of the former. The resurgent popularity of Manichaeism during the High Caliphate of Islam in the late eighth century, particularly within the Persian bureaucracy, stimulated the active responses of Islamic theologians.

Manichaeism is named for its prophet and founder, Mani, who was born of aristocratic Parthian parents in Mesopotamia in 216 CE. Mani's parents were members of one of the region's numerous baptist sects, probably the Elchasaites whose traditions some scholars trace to those of the ancient Qumran community in Palestine. Mani received his first revelation at the age of twelve. At twenty-four he received another, which called him to embark on his worldwide mission.

Mani began with a journey to Sind in northwestern India, where he is said to have converted a local Buddhist ruler to his new religion. Returning to Iran, he found an audience at the recently established Sasanian court. King Shapur I granted Mani the freedom to spread his teaching throughout Iran. The prophet's successes both at court and among the general population brought on the jealousy of the Zoroastrian magi, led by the chief priest Kerdir. The two remained rivals until the accession of Bahram I in 273, after which Kerdir succeeded in getting Mani expelled from favor. Mani died in prison in 276 at the age of sixty.

By comparison with other figures considered to be founders of major religions, Mani's career appears exceptionally deliberate and successful. He was a keen student of other religions and took from each what he found appropriate. Mani claimed to be a perfecter of Christianity, but his understanding of Jesus differed dramatically from that found in any Christian sect. He took from Zoroastrianism the commandment not to lie, along with much of its light symbolism and cosmic hierarchy. From Buddhism he borrowed the principle of non-injury, a belief in reincarnation, the notion of good deeds acquiring merit, and the quadripartite social structure of monastic and lay men and women. The Manichaean ideal of worldly poverty was common to both the Christian and Buddhist ascetic traditions. Mani taught Gnostic ideas such as the pairing of humans with their heavenly twins and the goal of ascension to a spiritual realm of light.

To say that Mani's was an intentionally syncretistic religion would probably be an understatement. In the *Kephalaia* he writes:

The writings, wisdoms, apocalypses, parables and psalms of the earlier churches are from all parts reunited in my church to the wisdom which I have revealed to you. As a river is joined to another river to form a powerful current, just so are the ancient books to my writings; and they form one great wisdom, such as has not existed in preceding generations.[2]

Mani preached in whatever terms were most familiar to his target audience, giving his message a Zoroastrian flavor when writing for the Sasanian king in the *Shabuhragan*, while presenting it as Christianity to Christians. Later Manichaean texts from Central Asia and China appear at first glance to be Buddhist. Mani explicitly enjoined his missionaries to take this "all things to all men" approach, borrowing the term "skillful means" directly from Mahayana Buddhism.

Mani also hoped to avoid sectarian squabbles and prevent any possible misunderstandings about his teaching from the very start. Seeing how Christians were battling over which texts to include in their canon and which to reject as spurious, he undertook to write his sacred scriptures by his own hand – seven in all. And realizing that in a world where most people were illiterate the texts themselves had limited immediate value, he used his considerable skill as a painter to illustrate a book for the visual embellishment of his teachings. Indeed, in Iran his reputation as an artist has outlived that as an arch-heretic; by the early seventeenth century one could find in a treatise on painting the statement that if one wished to applaud a brilliant painter, the highest of compliments was to compare him to Mani.[3]

Another effective strategy employed by Mani was to encourage his missionaries to translate his scriptures into vernacular languages. Judaism had been slow to do this, and eastern Christians used Syriac which was poorly understood or not at all by Iranians. Islam too would remain in many ways tied to the Arabic language.

Yet as part of the violent purges of Manichaeism under the Roman Empire in the West and later by the Islamic Caliphate in the East, all known Manichaean writings were destroyed. For many centuries the particulars of the religion were known only through the polemics of its enemies – St. Augustine, himself an ex-Manichaean, being the best known in the West – until archeological expeditions in the twentieth century turned up long-buried Manichaean libraries in the widely separated deserts of western China and Egypt. Since that time scholars have been busily translating and studying the newly discovered Manichaean texts and attempting to reconstruct the history, nature, and practice of this extinct world religion.

Virtually stamped out in the Roman Empire and vigorously persecuted by the Sasanians, Manichaeism moved east along the Silk Roads. Its main purveyors, as had been the case with Buddhism and Christianity, were Iranian merchants and monks who traveled with them. All three religions, lacking state sponsorship in many or most cases, relied heavily on the economic support of their respective monasteries which were located along the trade routes. Manichaean communities took hold in such places as Samarkand and further east in the Tarim basin, beyond the easy reach first of the Sasanians and then the Muslims, but the formal head of the Manichaean church remained at Baghdad.

Manichaeism enjoyed one and only one brief stint as official state religion, under a small state established by Uighur Turks in Central Asia from 763 to 840. Otherwise Manichaeans remained a distrusted minority wherever they were, from Iran to China, often outwardly professing to be good Muslims, Christians, Buddhists, or Taoists. The last Manichaean community appears to have survived in southeastern China into the seventeenth century, when it became unrecognizably absorbed into Buddhism. Scholars investigating a supposedly Buddhist temple in Fujian province during the late twentieth century were surprised to find a large number of Manichaean vessels and other objects, complete with inscriptions, as well as a statue in the shrine which identified itself as a representation of "Mani, the Buddha of Light."

## MANICHAEAN BELIEFS AND PRACTICES

The basic Manichaean worldview was one of Gnostic dualism, in which humans were seen as being entrapped in matter, estranged from their true home in the World of Light. How this predicament came about and how it may be escaped were elaborately explained through a retelling and reweaving of familiar myths drawn from Zoroastrianism, Judaism, and ancient Babylonia, along with Christian and Buddhist parables. As in other Gnostic systems, God – perceived as the Father of Light, and called Zurvan in some texts – was remote and unapproachable. Instead, humans dealt with a range of angels and demons, emanating either from the realm of Light or from that of Darkness.

As mentioned above, Manichaeism held Jesus to be a central figure, though it is a very different Jesus from that of the Christians. In fact the Manichaean Jesus has three aspects: he is Jesus the Splendor, the original purveyor of gnosis who imparts it to the First Man at the beginning of time and continues to bring esoteric knowledge to humans; he is the historical Jesus (though a docetic one – that is, only appearing to be human) whose suffering symbolizes the predicament of goodness being trapped as particles of light encased in matter; and he is Jesus the Judge who will come again at the end of time.

The following Manichaean hymn, translated from the Parthian language, speaks of the original entrapment of Light by an evil figure who, not accidentally, is a female:

Lo, that great Kingdom of Salvation [waits] on high,
Ready for those who have gnosis, so that they may finally find
    peace there.
Sinful, dark Pesus [the mother of the first humans] runs hither
    and thither brutishly,
She gives no peace at all to the upper and lower limbs [of Light];
She seizes and binds the Light in the six great bodies,
In earth, water and fire, wind, plants and animals.
She fashions it into many forms; she molds it into many
    figures;

She fetters it in a prison so that it may not ascend to the height.
She weaves [a net] around it on all sides, she piles it up;
She sets a watchman over it.
Greed and Lust are made its fellow captives [i.e., inside the
   human body].
She mixes destructive air into those six great bodies.
She nurtures her own body but destroys their sons.
The powers of Light on high confuse all the demons of wrath,
The sons of that Pesus, who is in a higher place.[4]

Several key themes are present in this hymn, including a feeling of
revulsion towards the body, and a negative attitude towards women
who are blamed for the process of reproduction which is seen as degen-
erative, insofar as it results in light particles being further diluted with
every generation. The Manichaean ideal was one of celibacy, or fail-
ing that, to practice the rhythm method when engaging in intercourse.
In practice this principle applied only to the monks (called "the Elect"),
however, since they required an ongoing succession of new generations of lay followers (called "Hearers") who could support them.

The same was true of the Buddhist community upon which that
of the Manichaeans was modeled, but the Manichaean case was more
extreme. The Elect, like Buddhist monks, were forbidden from
killing any living thing (they believed plants as well as animals had
souls), and they practiced vegetarianism as a lesser of evils. But even
so, the Elect were not to grow food, since disturbing the soil and
harvesting plants were thought to be damaging to the light particles
within them. They were not even to prepare their own food, but relied
on the Hearers to do this for them. Without a permanent and self-
regenerating community of lay supporters, Manichaeism, like Buddhism, would have died out within a generation. Though Hearers could
not hope for immediate salvation, they could aspire to be reborn as
members of the Elect.

Given the dependence of the monks on the laity for their very survival, it is not surprising that the daily ritual meal was the central
component of Manichaean practice. The most important event of the
Manichaean calendar, furthermore, was the feast of Bema, which
commemorated Mani's death and fulfilled a similar function to that
of Easter in Christianity. Paintings from manuscripts and monastery

walls in the Turfan region of western China depict these ritual meals in a way which bears a striking resemblance to those practiced by Zoroastrians today.

While much of contemporary Manichaean studies has focused on the cosmology and corresponding mythologies present in the recently discovered Manichaean texts, Jason BeDuhn has emphasized the action-based aspects of Manichaean practice, pointing out that the Manichaean lifestyle was more than merely a withdrawal from a disgusting world of material bondage. Rather, the aim of Manichaeans' life in this world was to strive actively to liberate particles of light through their rituals and practices.

The proper use of food was a primary means of doing this. By purifying themselves through their rigorously regimented daily lives, and thus separating out the evil which clung to them like tarnish on a silver vessel, the Manichaean Elect were thought capable of freeing the light particles within food by the very process of eating it. Fresh, uncooked produce was favored as possessing the highest proportion of light. St. Augustine ridicules Manichaean beliefs about food – what BeDuhn calls "metabolic salvation" – in the following passage:

> All you promise (the Hearers) is not a resurrection, but a change to another mortal existence, in which they shall live the life of your Elect, the life you live yourself, and are so much praised for; or if they are worthy of the better they shall enter into melons and cucumbers, or some food which will be chewed, that they may quickly be purified by your belches.[5]

This is propaganda, of course. According to the Manichaean texts, the Elect sent up the liberated light not in the form of "belches," but as hymns sung during and after the meal.

What was the appeal of Manichaeism, which brought so many converts from so many different cultural backgrounds to adopt its austere worldview? Its esoteric cosmology and teaching could hardly have been accessible to large numbers from among the general population. Mani himself must have been a highly charismatic figure, as must some of his missionaries. They welcomed debates with proponents of other religions, but how did they win these debates?

While the persuasion of rhetoric and reason must have played some role, it would appear that other skills such as magic and healing were often instrumental in winning converts. Western Asia had long been home to a confusing plethora of religious sects, and historical accounts from all periods make mention of religious leaders who amaze people with miracles of one kind or another. Jesus of Nazareth is one well-known example, but similar claims are made about virtually all religious figures with popular appeal.

Like Jesus, Mani was known as a miracle-worker and a physician. Indeed, during his years at the royal court he seems to have been valued more for his medical knowledge than for his spiritual insights. A Manichaean church history in Sogdian tells of how one of Mani's disciples, Gabryab, challenged the King of Revan (possibly Yerevan in Armenia) to see whether the Christians at court could heal a sick girl:

> If I through the mercy of the Gods can heal the girl of the illness, then I shall require this of you: "Turn away from the Christian religion, and accept the religion of the Lord Mar Mani!" At that he turned around and said to the Christians: "Christ was a god who could work miracles. The blind as well as the lame and cripples he healed of their disease. Similarly he also revived the dead. And it is a rule, that the son has the traits of the father and that the pupil shows the mark of the teacher. If you really and truly are disciples of Christ, and the mark and trait of Christ are upon you, then all come here and cure the girl of her disease, just as Jesus said to the disciples: 'Where you lay your hand, there will I work improvement through God's hand!' If you do not do so, then I by God's power shall heal the girl of the disease, and then you Christians shall go from the kingdom of Revan." The Christians said: "We will not be able to heal her; you make the girl healthy instead."[6]

Gabryab, of course, succeeds in healing the girl, and the king becomes a Manichaean. Once Gabryab moves on, however, the devious Christians persuade the king to return to Christianity.

OPPOSITION TO MANICHAEISM

Of all the religions competing for the devotion of Iranians in the third century, Manichaeism was clearly considered by the Zoroastrian magi to be the greatest threat. This may have been partly to do with the direct personal rivalry of Mani and Kerdir, but presumably popular response played a role as well. For the Zoroastrian priests Manichaeism became the epitome of heresy. Indeed, the generic term they used for heretic, *zindiq*, originally meant "Manichaean." This usage, which was mirrored in Byzantine Christendom, continued into Islamic times.

Among the texts composed by Zoroastrian priests to refute Manichaean doctrines, one of the most significant is found in the *Denkard*. In this work the priests list twelve specific points on which Manichaeism and Zoroastrianism are fundamentally at odds. These points include such central doctrines as the essence of human nature – Zoroastrians believed people to be basically good, while Manichaeans believed the opposite – and a rejection of the world, which Zoroastrians believed was created by Ahura Mazda to be perfected, whereas Manichaeans believed it was created out of evil, that it cannot be otherwise, and that it must be escaped. Another point of difference was their respective views of agriculture, which Zoroastrians saw as life-giving and Manichaeans as life- [that is, light-] destroying. Zoroastrians saw the material world as infused with good spirits (*mainyu*s) which should be drawn into oneself; Manichaeans saw these as evils to be expelled. Zoroastrians shunned celibacy, while Manichaeans celebrated it. Of course, the argument in the *Denkard* is constructed in terms of the Zoroastrian understanding of Manichaean doctrines, which may have been less than accurate.

Manichaeism posed a somewhat different danger to Islam than it did to Zoroastrianism and Christianity. Despite their religion's possession of sacred scriptures, Manichaeans were never granted the protected status of "peoples of the book." The Arab Umayyads (661–750) seem to have paid little attention to Manichaeism, as to other religions practiced among non-Arab subject populations. A rise in anti-Manichaean literature shortly after this period suggests that Manichaeism was spreading, however. With the geographical shift of the Caliphate to the Iranian world under the Abbasids from 750 and the need of the new government to suppress the kind of heterodox forces that had helped bring them to power, Manichaeism came to be seen as a major threat.

Muslim theologians, following earlier critiques by Christian writers, accused the Manichaeans of being unwilling to interpret their fantastic cosmogonic myths allegorically – a position we today might associate with what we call "religious fundamentalism." Muslim philosophers, steeped in the tradition of Aristotle and other classical thinkers, disputed what they believed to be the Manichaeans' rejection of accidents and potentiality. Muslims claimed that the Manichaeans did not believe in spirits, but only in what they could experience through their senses, and that they believed the Father of Light is the very same light which is perceived in this world.

One of the major theological debates in monotheistic religions arises from the problem of evil – how a single creator god can be both all-powerful and entirely good – and the consequent problem of whether humans possess free will or are predestined to act as they do. Manichaeans, like other dualists, had a much easier time dealing with these issues, since they posited that evil was due to the interference of an evil deity. Some scholars have argued that the free-will debate among Muslims, which took shape under the Mu'tazilite school in the eighth century, began as an effort to refute the Manichaeans.[7]

Manichaeans operated secretively during Islamic times, and apparently had considerable success either in converting Muslims or in keeping non-Muslim Iranians away from Islam. They are known to have circulated a number of false *hadith*s (reports) about the prophet Muhammad as part of their propaganda. In the eighth and ninth centuries a sort of dualism seems to have become popular among the literate bureaucratic classes of Iran as a form of nationalist reassertion against the ruling Arabs, but it is hard to know if what they practiced was Manichaeism as such or some other kind of Iranian dualistic "heresy" such as Mazdakism.

### Later esoteric movements

Certain aspects of Gnosticism have reappeared throughout history in all manner of Iranian religious behaviors, from resistance movements such as the Mazdakites or the Babakites (discussed below), to underground sects such as the Isma'ili Shi'is, to the elitist speculations of the Hellenistically inspired philosophers Avicenna, Shehab al-din Sohravardi and others, and to the mystical teachings of various Sufis. None of these later expressions possesses the extreme anti-materialism of Manichaeism, though they all share to some degree Manichaeism's dualistic cosmology and its symbolism of light as a representative of goodness, purity, and the divine.

One of the most severe magi-led persecutions of religions other than Zoroastrianism during the Sasanian period occurred under King Peroz I (r. 459–487). During this time the Kanthaeans (Arabic *kaynaniyya* or *kanthawiyya*), a Gnostic-baptist sect in Persian Babylonia possibly related to the Mandaeans, sought to protect themselves by adopting Zoroastrian rituals associated with fire temples. Their leader, a priest named Battai, changed his own name to the more Zoroastrian-sounding Yazdani. The Kanthaeans seem to have adapted several Manichaean texts and rituals for their own use. They survived into Islamic times and apparently participated in theological debates with Muslims. Like the Manichaeans, some of them practiced vegetarianism and celibacy, and believed in the transmigration of souls.

The early sixth-century religious reform movement led by Mazdak (which he called the *drust-din*, the "right religion") seems to have arisen some time earlier under the leadership of a priestly figure calling himself Zarodosht (Zoroaster). The Kanthaeans, who were numerous in the region where Mazdak was born, may also have influenced him in some respects. Yet Mazdak seems to have presented himself as simply a reformer of the official Zoroastrianism, able to detect "hidden, inner meanings" in the Zoroastrian texts.

All the surviving textual evidence about Mazdak's movement is from external, antagonistic sources, mainly later Muslim ones. According to the poetically embellished tenth-century account in the *Shah-nameh* of Ferdowsi, Mazdak originally held a government post as keeper of the treasury. Seeing that much of society's ills were due to people being in want, he ordered the granaries opened and their contents freely distributed. The king, Kavad I (r. 488–531), was swayed by Mazdak's message of justice, but Prince Khosrow, the future king Anushirvan, was not. According to Ferdowsi, Mazdak offered Khosrow the following explanation of the world:

There are five things which turn wise men from the truth. They are envy, anger, hatred, and the needs which are usually followed by greed. If you overcome these five *div*s [demons], the path of the Lord of the Universe will emerge clearly before you. The incitements to these five are worldly possessions and women. It is because of this that the Good Religion [*beh-din*; i.e., Zoroastrianism] has waned in the world. If you wish to avert harm from the Good Religion, women and possessions must be shared in common.[8]

In Ferdowsi's version of the story, after six months Prince Khosrow organizes an inter-faith debate (which includes a Christian bishop) during which the Zoroastrian chief priest persuades the king to renounce the faith of Mazdak, who is then hanged from the gallows.

While Ferdowsi's account is not history, other sources suggest the backdrop of the incident he describes, which probably occurred in the 520s. At this time there were two major rival factions at the Sasanian court looking to the eventual succession of the aged king Kavad. Mazdak's supporters favored the king's eldest son, Kavus, but the party supporting Khosrow eventually prevailed. Khosrow Anushirvan went on to become one of pre-Islamic Iran's most celebrated rulers and is credited with initiating an important series of social reforms. These reforms, however, may have come at least partly in response to the injustices and inequalities that had made so many Iranians supportive of Mazdak's teachings.

What little that is known of Mazdak's religious doctrines comes mainly from later Muslim sources. Mazdak retained the dualism and light symbolism of Manichaeism, but according to the Muslim heresiographer Shahrestani (1076–1153), Mazdak's system differed from Manichaeism mainly in that he believed that Light (goodness) works freely and deliberately, whereas Darkness (evil) works at random. Yet salvation is by chance, not choice. This notion, which resembles in some ways that of sudden enlightenment in Zen Buddhism, was anti-elitist, in that even the lowliest person might fortuitously receive it. Like the Manichaeans, the Mazdakites were urged to practice vegetarianism, but unlike them they condoned suicide as an escape from the material world.

In 750 a Khorasan-based rebel movement of Arab settlers and local Iranians, generally referred to as the "Abbasid revolution," toppled the Arab Umayyad dynasty. While ostensibly Shi'ite in its ideology, the movement had undercurrents of Mazdakism. The rebellion was led by an Iranian general known as Abu Muslim, whose charisma and success made him a threat to the very people he had brought to power. The Abbasid movement included a wide range of groups, both Muslim and non-Muslim, who shared a hatred for the ruling Umayyads as well as a tendency to extremist beliefs (Arabic *ghuluw*).

Once in power the new Abbasid government executed Abu Muslim in 753, but his non-Muslim followers believed he would be reincarnated and they maintained their allegiance to him after his death. In Shahrestani's time (i.e., the twelfth century) there were still what could be considered Mazdakite communities scattered throughout Iran and Central Asia, among which Shahrestani counts those he calls "Abu Muslimiyya." Mazdakite groups thus continued to revere Abu Muslim and his descendants for several centuries.

Two major Mazdakite revolts against Abbasid rule occurred in the wake of Abu Muslim's execution. The first, which was quickly put down, rallied behind a general named Sunbad who claimed that Abu Muslim's spirit had entered his body. A second rebellion took place in Central Asia under the leadership of a self-proclaimed prophet known as al-Muqanna', "the Veiled One." Al-Muqanna', who kept the Abbasid authorities at bay from 777 to 786, is described by later Muslim sources as instructing his followers to practice Mazdak's religion.

A Mazdakism-influenced leader named Babak, based in northern Iran, led a rebellion against the Abbasid government beginning in 816. From Babak's time the religion was known as the *khurram-din* or "happy religion," in keeping with Mazdak's teaching of a joyful and generous approach to life. They denied the Day of Judgment and considered that final authority in all matters of belief lay in the esoteric interpretations of the leader of the sect. Their rituals centered on purity and included the use of bread and wine.

Anticipating approaches such as that of the Baha'is in the nineteenth century and the perennial philosophers of the twentieth, the Khurramis believed that all religions were basically true and that all prophets bring messages from the same source. They assumed that all religious people were essentially on the right path, as long as they did not harm the community of the Khurramis. (This condition allowed the otherwise pacifist Khurramis to kill many thousands of their

Muslim persecutors.) They were said to be peaceful and cheerful except when in battle, and their ethical approach could be expressed as "do as you will but harm none." Though some (but only some) may have practiced free love, this was apparently done only with the consent of the women involved.

Babak's revolt seriously destabilized the Caliphate for many years until his eventual capture and execution in 837. Although Babak's followers continued to stage occasional rebellions, the movement was greatly weakened, and over time the followers of Mazdakite doctrines became absorbed in diverse esoteric Muslim groups. Lacking a clear leader, many later Mazdakites came to look to the Isma'ili Shi'i imams as their source of guidance and authority.

Iranian Gnosticism continued to exist, but in Islamic garb. Isma'ili Shi'ism would draw on much of the symbolism of pre-Islamic gnosis, as would illuminationist philosophy and some Iranian Sufi mystical traditions. The Sufi notion of *erfan* (gnosis), understood as sublime insight acquired through a combination of personal discipline and divine grace, has long held an attraction for Iranian Muslim mystics, and is now even studied in the seminaries of Qom as an academic subject.

In 1844 an English missionary, Joseph Wolff, met a group of Persian Sufis while traveling in Central Asia. "The time will come," they told him, "when there shall be no difference between rich and poor, between high and low, when property shall be in common – even wives and children."[9] Hidden beneath a veneer of Islamic mysticism, the social platform of Mazdak had survived for thirteen centuries!

# 7

# ISLAM

During the middle decades of the seventh century an army of Arabs, united for the first time by a new faith, Islam, stunned both the Roman (Byzantine) and Persian (Sasanian) empires by conquering the important Byzantine provinces of Egypt and Syria and the whole of the Sasanian realm. The Arabian peninsula, which was mostly sparsely inhabited desert, had never before been a region of political importance. The great empires only concerned themselves with controlling the coastal regions, where there were a number of towns which served as staging posts along the trade routes that linked the Mediterranean with the Indian Ocean. These towns had often been under the economic hegemony of Iran, and most were home to small Iranian trading communities.

Iranians thus had a long presence in Arabia, where prior to Islam there were expatriate groups of Zoroastrians, Manichaeans, and Mazdakites. At the same time some Arabs, especially among the Tamim tribe, practiced Zoroastrianism. One of the first Meccan converts to Muhammad's new religion was a man known as Salman al-Farsi ("the Persian"). It was an Iranian slave, Firuz, who murdered the second Caliph Umar ibn al-Khattab.

It is clear that neither the Persians nor the Romans had ever considered the Arabs to be a serious threat. Arabian society was extremely diffuse. Largely pastoral nomadic, it was made up of clans who could enter into pacts with each other but lacked any central organization. Muhammad of Mecca, who began receiving divine revelations in the year 610 at the age of forty, was the first Arab to win the allegiance of all the clans of the Arabian peninsula.

Muhammad's prophetic career did not get off to an easy start. The revelations he preached in Mecca posed a challenge to many of the city's inhabitants. His vision of monotheism was uncompromisingly radical – even the Christian trinity appeared to him as a kind of polytheism. Mecca, being a trading town, had temples to the various religions of local expatriate business communities, and pious donations were an important part of the local economy. Muhammad also preached a powerful social critique, warning that those who did not practice charity and justice would be judged by God for their acts. Since in Muhammad's time social disparities seem to have been on the rise, his message was unwelcome among Mecca's wealthy and powerful elites.

Though Muhammad does not seem to have had direct contact with any Iranian religious community, Iranian ideas were part of Arab culture and as such are present in the Qur'an. Islamic beliefs in heaven and hell, a last judgment based on the weighing (*mizan*) of good and bad deeds, a bridge of death, and angels, as well as tendencies towards millenarianism, messianism, and apocalypticism, along with notions of ritual purity, have all been argued to have Iranian origins. The five daily prayers (Arabic *salat*, Persian *namaz*), which became the most visible expression of Islamic piety, mirror ancient Zoroastrian practice. The popular Muslim story of Muhammad's miraculous night journey to heaven (the *mi'raj*) is paralleled in the Middle Persian tale of Arda Viraz, which may also be the ultimate source for Dante's *Divine Comedy*. The Islamic belief that Jesus' death on the cross was mere appearance derives from Manichaeism, as does the Islamic tithe for charity (*zakat*). The angels Harut and Marut (Qur'an 2:96) are reflections of the Zoroastrian Haurvatat and Ameretat. The Qur'an mentions Zoroastrians (*al-majus*) alongside Jews, Christians, and Sabeans as true "believers in Revelation," in contrast to followers of idol-worshipping faiths (Qur'an 22:17). The Qur'anic Arabic language includes a number of Persian loanwords.

The ongoing revelations transmitted by Muhammad in his hometown of Mecca attracted a growing number of followers, largely among the disenfranchised of the city. Eventually tensions reached a point where Muhammad felt compelled to accept an offer from the inhabitants of Yathrib, an agricultural town several days' journey to the north, to bring his group to live there. This migration, called the *hijra* in Arabic, marks the beginning of the Islamic calendar in 622 CE.

From his new base in Yathrib, which came to be known as *Madinat al-nabi* ("the City of the Prophet") or Medina for short, Muhammad and his companions were able to launch raids against the caravans of Meccans and build up their economic and political strength. Raiding was an accepted part of the economic life all throughout the marginally productive Arabian peninsula, hence the prevalence of pacts by which weaker clans would seek the support of stronger ones. As Muhammad's community grew in power, one by one the clans of Arabia sent emissaries to seek such agreements.

The traditional act of submission by the weak to the powerful, which is called *islam* in Arabic, can be read as having either a political or religious significance in Muhammad's case, since it is impossible to know whether the Arabs felt they were submitting to Muhammad's authority as leader of his group or to the authority of the one God, Allah, whose prophet he claimed to be. One may suspect that for many of the Arabs it may have been the former, since Arabic accounts of what translators have called "conversions" indicate that people generally "submitted" (*aslamu*) first, then only afterwards learned about the Qur'an, its content, and the social codes of the Muslims. This is true not only of the initial period but of conversions throughout the early centuries of the Islamic Caliphate.

Another fact which supports the theory that the socio-political definition of *islam* precedes the religious one, is that once word went out of Muhammad's death in 632 many of the Arab tribes rebelled. But by that time Muhammad's community, the *umma*, was strong enough that the recalcitrant Arabs were brought once again under the control of his successor (*khalifa*, or Caliph), Abu Bakr.

With the entire peninsula bound by mutual allegiance to the *umma*, it was no longer possible for the Arabs to raid each other. Quite naturally, they therefore extended their raids to neighboring lands. Their unprecedented empowerment, buttressed by a new faith and combined with the weakness, exhaustion, and unpopularity of the Roman and Persian regimes, enabled the Arabs to expand their rule from Spain to the frontiers of China and India within only a few decades.

From a religious point of view Arab rule was also far less oner-
ous for its subjects than the Roman or the Persian governments had
been. For centuries each of the imperial states had sponsored one
officially recognized religion – Chalcedonian Christianity in the case
of the Romans and Zoroastrianism in the case of the Persians – and
allowed their established clergies to wage continuous campaigns
against any sect they deemed heretical. The Arabs, by contrast,
allowed individual communities to run their own affairs and follow
their own customs, requiring only that they pay a poll tax, the *jizya*,
which was less than the extortionate taxes that had been extracted
by previous regimes. For followers of minority or heterodox religious
sects, this release from the persecution of ruthless magi or intolerant
bishops must have come as an enormous relief.

During the first several centuries of Muslim rule in Iran the
authority of the Zoroastrian priests slowly but steadily eroded.
Their state support forever lost, the magi had to compete financially
– subsisting as they did on fees charged for the performance of rituals and ceremonies – with Muslim governments who were levying
the poll tax and other obligations on Zoroastrian citizens.

It may also be that in aligning their interests with those of the
Sasanian government more than with the general population, the magi
had ceased to serve the spiritual needs of many Iranians. The widespread popularity in Iran of Christianity, Manichaeism, and, in the
east, of Buddhism, as well as the ease with which new movements
such as that of Mazdak won large followings, can be taken as further evidence that the Zoroastrian priests had dangerously distanced
themselves from the requirements of the general population.

## From "the religion of the Arabs" to universal faith system

Richard Bulliet has suggested, based on his reading of family
genealogies from Khorasan, that by the year 1000 about eighty percent of urban Iranians (albeit in a largely rural society) were
Muslim. Why so many Zoroastrians, Christians, Jews, Buddhists, and
others chose to embrace the new faith is open to consideration.
Presumably many factors played a role.

Forced conversion was *not* one of these factors, during the early
period at least. The Arabs initially saw their surprising successes as

a sign that God had favored them above all other peoples, and they were not for the most part overly eager to share the fruits of those successes too widely. The conversions of subject peoples throughout the period of the Damascus-based Umayyad dynasty (661–749 CE) appear to have been mainly a case of Arab society being overwhelmed by the popular demand of outsiders for inclusion in the privileged class. This led to tensions as non-Arab converts came to outnumber Arab Muslims, a transition which probably occurred by the early eighth century.

For the many peoples who had come under Arab rule, Arabian social norms constituted the formal basis for relations between the Arabs and their subject communities. Islam was initially perceived both by the Arabs and by their subjects as "the Arab religion" (*din al-'arab* in the sources), so "converting" to Islam literally entailed "going Arab." Because Arab society was based on blood ties, it was necessary for any non-Arab who wanted to join the Muslim community to find an Arab patron, who could give him a sort of honorary membership in a particular Arab clan. Obviously this gave the patron a certain amount of leverage over his client (*mawla*, pl. *mawali*), and non-Arab converts often felt that despite the Qur'an's universalist message they were still being treated as second-class citizens. The growing disaffection of non-Arab converts merged with that of certain marginalized Arab clans, eventually giving rise to the so-called "Abbasid" movement which successfully challenged the ruling hierarchy. The ideology chosen by the rebels to symbolize their struggle was drawn from an event that occurred before Muhammad's death in 632 CE.

## CHALLENGING THE BASIS OF TEMPORAL AUTHORITY

The passing away of God's Messenger brought about the first major crisis within the Muslim community. Muhammad's friend and father-in-law Abu Bakr, a man who by all accounts was widely respected, is said to have emerged from Muhammad's tent and told the anxious crowd, "If any among you worshipped Muhammad then let it be known that he is gone. But if you worship God then know that He is eternal and never dies." Still, as transmitter of the divine revelation of the Qur'an, Muhammad's leadership had been vital and unquestioned. The problem of how the community was to decide on a successor was left unresolved, at least in the minds of many.

For others the issue had been settled during Muhammad's lifetime. Muslims generally agree that at a place called Ghadir Khumm, he had taken Ali, his nephew and son-in-law (Ali was married to Muhammad's only surviving child, Fatima), by the hand in a traditional performative gesture and declared that "whatever I am the master of, Ali is the master of." Most of those present assumed he meant his own household. A significant minority, however, understood him to mean he was designating Ali as his successor as leader of the Muslims. These were the *Shi'at 'Ali*, or "partisans of Ali" – better known as the Shi'ites.

But at the time of Muhammad's death, the majority of his followers sought to resolve the issue of succession through the traditional means of their society. Umar ibn al-Khattab, considered by many to be a contender for the role, preempted any dispute by taking Abu Bakr's hand in a formal gesture of allegiance and proclaiming his support for him. But those who felt that Muhammad had already chosen his successor were not satisfied, feeling that Ali had been unjustly deprived of his rightful position as leader of the Muslims. Ali himself seems to have held this view, though he did not protest at the time.

Eventually Ali was chosen to be the fourth Caliph, but the powerful Umayyad family, based in Damascus, refused to acknowledge his authority. Eventually, having agreed to arbitration with his rivals, in 661 Ali was murdered by a disgruntled faction of his own followers. His eldest son, Hasan, declined the leadership role Ali's supporters expected of him, and Ali's younger son Husayn stepped in. Buttressed by what appeared to be strong support in southern Iraq, Husayn challenged the rule of the Syria-based Umayyads. But when the Umayyad Caliph Yazid sent an army to put down the rebellion, Husayn found himself abandoned by all but a handful of supporters and was killed by Yazid's forces at Karbala in 680 CE. In the years that followed there arose a tendency for anyone in Muslim society who had any cause to feel marginalized – whether professionally, socially, politically, or otherwise – to see in the murders of Ali and his son Husayn a symbol for all those who had suffered injustice of whatever kind.

By the mid-eighth century the majority non-Arab Muslims of eastern Iran, in alliance with Arab garrisons who chafed at having been relegated to the backwaters of the empire, were strong enough to challenge the ruling Umayyads, whom they collectively viewed as corrupt and un-Islamic despots. Led by a charismatic Iranian general known as Abu Muslim, the rebels rallied in the name of a descendant of Muhammad's uncle Abbas, seeking to put him at the head of the Caliphate. In 751 CE they succeeded in overthrowing the Umayyads, and the "Abbasid" empire was born.

## The Iranian role in shaping Islamic civilization

From the first contact between the Arab Muslims and the Iranian population there were intermarriages between the two, especially between the daughters of important Iranian families and the sons of Arab ones. Conquering armies almost always take the womenfolk of those they have vanquished, but in this case such marriages served a double purpose. For the Arabs, alliances with Iranian families helped improve their prestige among a subject people that still saw themselves as possessing the superior civilization. For Iranians, marital alliances were a way of holding on to their status and privilege under changed political circumstances. It is easy to forget that the children of such marriages would have grown up far more Iranianized than is apparent on the surface. There is a prevalent male fiction that fathers determine their children's education, but women know better. The role of Iranian mothers in maintaining and passing on Iranian cultural traditions after the Arab conquest is rarely documented but was certainly significant.

What is far better attested is the predominance of Iranian men in working out all aspects of what would become the universal Islamic civilization, whether in law, theology, science, philosophy, history, geography, the arts, even in the realm of Arabic literature and linguistics. Although the Arabs brought peoples as diverse as Egyptians, Syrians, Greeks, Berbers, Visigoths, and Indians under their far-flung administration, none of these peoples or their cultures would contribute as much to the emerging world of Islam as the Iranians. Indeed within a little over a century Iranians would come to play a larger role than the Arabs themselves.

With the overthrow of the Umayyads in 751 the leaders of the Abbasid movement chose to move the capital eastward, closer to their Iranian power base. After initially establishing themselves at Kufa in Iraq, they built a new city near the former Persian capital of Ctesiphon between the Tigris and Euphrates rivers. They called their new capital Baghdad, a Persian word meaning "given by God."

With the Muslim world's center of gravity now shifted to the fringes of Iran, the new government soon took on the role of successors to the pre-Islamic Sasanians.[1] While the Umayyad administration had been in many respects a somewhat superficially Arabized continuation of the provincial Byzantine government of Syria, the Abbasids adopted the institutional apparatus of the Sasanians. The system of governmental departments (*divan*) including the office of prime minister (*vazir*), the postal and intelligence service (*barid*), and the tax farming system of the landowners (*dehqan*s) were kept more or less intact. The court system, in which judges (*qadi*s) were appointed from among the scholars of religious law, was a continuation of the Sasanian model. At first the Abbasid coins placed Arabic inscriptions next to images of Zoroastrian fire altars. Sasanian court traditions such as poetry and music were maintained and embellished by Arab influences. The Abbasids kept the Persian solar calendar and the equinox festivals of Noruz and Mehregan, and adopted the Sasanian ideology of kingship whereby the ruler was considered to be the "Shadow of God on Earth" (*zillu-llah fi'l-ard*), a thoroughly un-Arab and un-Islamic notion. Finally, they dispensed with any lingering threats from their own rebellious past by initiating a persecution of Shi'ites.

The door was opened to Iranian influence in every aspect of Muslim life and society. Both the codification of Islamic law and the collation of *hadith*s – reports about the words and deeds of Muhammad, which served as one of the basic sources of Islamic jurisprudence – occurred mainly in the Iranian cultural sphere. The compilers of all six collections of hadiths considered canonical by later Sunnis (that is, the majority of the world's Muslims) were scholars of Iranian background. The very impulse for collecting hadiths was due to the emergence of a whole new set of conflicts over how to order and maintain Muslim society, a society which was no longer monocultural but had become thoroughly cosmopolitan.

As long as the majority of Muslims had been Arabs, traditional Arabian cultural norms continued to be accepted wherever they were not altered or abrogated by the divine revelation of the Qur'an. And indeed, throughout the first century of the Islamic period under the Umayyad dynasty, descendants of the Arabs who had originally submitted to Muhammad's authority took this approach, resolving legal disputes through the "informed opinion" (*ray*) of an appointed judge, who was usually an Arab.

Once Arabs were in the minority, however, other sets of long-established social norms began to compete with Arab ones. If an answer could not be found in the Qur'an, the next recourse was to claim that one's position was vindicated in an example of Muhammad. Obviously it was possible to invent stories in which Muhammad was said to have done this or that, and such inventions quickly became rampant. It was urgent for Muslims to find a way to authenticate stories about their prophet which could be used as a basis for establishing a universal social code. This project, which resulted in the formulation of *shari'a* law, took at least two centuries, and it took place largely in the Iranian world.

The early Abbasid period is known as "the Classical Age of Islam," and in this time Iranian scholars were everywhere preeminent. Famous figures such as the historians Tabari and Miskawayh, the mathematician Khwarazmi, the physician-philosophers Rhazes and Avicenna, the geographers Ebn Khordadbeh, Estakhri and Ebn al-Faqih, and the Sufi theologian Ghazali, were all Iranians.

In the realm of language and literature Iranians again played a central role. That an Iranian, Sibawayh, should have been the first to write down a systematic grammar of Arabic is no surprise. Arabs didn't need grammars – it was the Iranians who had to learn Arabic as a foreign language. As Iranian intellectuals sought to express their ideas in this new tongue, they found that many abstract philosophical or technical terms did not exist in Arabic and had to be invented. Neologisms were coined using the Iranians' analysis of the grammatical rules of Arabic.

Beginning in the mid-eighth century, a group of mainly Iranian scribes called the *sho'obiyyeh* (literally, "the gentiles") translated many literary works from Middle Persian (Pahlavi) into Arabic, both for the benefit of their Arab superiors and to ensure a wider distribution throughout the empire. Perhaps too, in bringing so many classics back to life, there was a sense of asserting Persian cultural superiority. "Mirrors for Princes" type literature such as the *Book of Governance* (*Kitab al-sahaba*) helped to shape the Abbasid concept of rule, while semi-legendary royal chronicles like the *Book of Kings* (*Khwaday namag*, the main model for Ferdowsi's later epic rendition, the *Shah-nameh*) provided the historical framework into which Islamic rulers sought to situate themselves. Morality tales such as the animal fables of *Kalila and Dimna* and the adventure stories of *The Tales of A Thousand and One Nights*, of Indian provenance but best known in their Middle Persian versions, served both to entertain and instruct. Thus was the Sasanian literary tradition assimilated into the Islamic world.

Another form of Iranian reassertion which existed at this time, especially among the bureaucratic elites, took the form of crypto-religion. The best-known of the *sho'obiyyeh*, Rozbeh son of Dadoy, called Ibn al-Muqaffa', was perhaps a typical case. A government employee, his conversion to Islam was clearly opportunistic, and eventually he was accused of being an infidel and executed. Large numbers of Iranian intellectuals at the time secretly practiced some form of esoteric Iranian religion – the term used, *zandaqa*, usually meant "Manichaeism" but could refer to any dualistic heresy – which brought about a major official purge of suspected heretics. The movement was crushed under the Caliph al-Mahdi from 775–785, but reemerged in altered form during the following century in the form of various Shi'ite beliefs which spread among the same class of literate Iranians.

Throughout the first two centuries of Arab domination various resistance movements throughout Iran took on a religious character. One such attempt to throw off Arab rule was led by the magician Muqanna' in Central Asia in the 780s. The best-known, however (and in the Islamic sources, the most abhorred), was the rebellion of Babak in northern Iran from 816–837, discussed earlier.

Though these and other attempts to resist Arab domination ultimately failed, Iranian culture did succeed in reasserting itself throughout the tenth century as the eastern provinces of the empire, first the governors of Khorasan and then those of Seistan further south, successively freed themselves from many aspects of the Caliphate's centralized rule. Written Persian, which had given way to Arabic for two centuries, began to reemerge and finally regained its status as official language under the Samanid dynasty of Central Asia (875–998 CE).

The major type of institution for the propagation of Islamic higher learning, the *madrasa* (literally "place of study"), arose in Iran during the tenth and eleventh centuries. By the time the Seljuk prime minister Nezam al-Molk (himself an Iranian) built the famous Nezamiyyeh madrasa in Baghdad in 1063, there were already some twenty-five madrasas functioning in Iran. The madrasas, with their regularized curriculum based on law and hadith studies, were the primary mechanism through which a normative Sunni Islam was developed and disseminated throughout the Muslim world.

## Isma'ili Shi'ism in Iran

Following the massacre of Muhammad's grandson Husayn and his followers at Karbala in 680 CE, Shi'ism became an underground movement subject to constant persecution by the Umayyad and Abbasid governments. Faced with the real danger of extermination, Shi'is developed a doctrine of dissimulation (*taqiyya*) by which they could outwardly profess Sunni Islam while secretly adhering to the divinely inspired authority and guidance of the descendants of Muhammad known as the Imams. The existing pattern continued, whereby those disaffected with the ruling regime tended to find in the martyrdoms of Ali and Husayn a powerful symbol for all manner of oppression and injustice faced by God's true believers.

Since Shi'is believed that the divine inspiration and infallible status of the rightful leader of all Muslims was given to only one person at any given time, with the death of each successive Imam there arose inevitable disagreements over who was next in line. The majority of Shi'is agree on the identity of the first six Imams, but following the death of Ja'far al-Sadiq in 764 CE there was a major split. Some followed the line of his elder son Isma'il, who had been the designated heir but predeceased his father, while others believed that authority had passed to his younger son Musa al-Kazim. The latter faction continued to follow a line up to the Twelfth Imam, Muhammad al-Mahdi, whom they believe went into occultation in 873 CE (he is subsequently referred to as the Hidden Imam) and will return as a messianic figure at the end of time. This group became known as the "Twelver" (*Ithna 'Ashari*) Shi'is.

The first group, who followed the line of Isma'il, trace the descent of living Imams right up to the present day. The present Aga Khan, a man known for supporting charitable causes throughout the Muslim world, is revered by Isma'ili or "Sevener" Muslims today as the Imam of the Age. For Isma'ilis, the living Imam is the unique possessor of an esoteric knowledge that enables him to perceive the hidden meanings beneath outward signs (such as the verses of the Qur'an). For this reason their opponents have often referred to them by the derisive label *batiniyya*, meaning "esotericists."

The tenth century is sometimes referred to by historians as "the Shi'ite century," since much of the Muslim world at that time had come under the rule of Shi'ite dynasties. In Egypt a band of Sevener Shi'ites originally from the region of Libya ruled under the name of the Fatimids (909–1171 CE), challenging the legitimacy of the Sunni Caliph in Baghdad. The latter post itself became something of a figurehead position, as a Shi'ite group from the north of Iran, known as the Buwayhids or Buyids (932–1062 CE), asserted their military control over Baghdad and effectively took over the reins of government.

During this period some recently Islamicized Turkic tribes from Central Asia – first the Ghaznavids (from 977) and then the Seljuks (from 1038) – were also using their positions as mercenaries in the Caliph's army to vie for power over the Islamic heartlands. The Turks found in the now embattled Sunni Islam an ideology by which they could rally support among the still largely Sunni population, in opposition to both the Fatimid and Buyid ruling classes. The Turks prevailed in Baghdad, driving the Buyids from power, then launched an all-out campaign against the Egyptian Fatimids. The Fatimids aggravated the Seljuk Turks by sending waves of Isma'ili missionaries to proselytize throughout the Seljuk-controlled territories of Meso-potamia and Iran.

The Isma'ili belief system was drawn from a combination of Islamic sources, Hellenistic philosophy, and Iranian mysticism of light, even some subtle borrowings from Manichaean myth. Isma'ili esotericism already had a foothold among the Iranian intellectual classes, as men-tioned earlier. Iranian Isma'ilis, who were seen as a fifth column by the Seljuks, maintained contact with the Fatimids and occasionally traveled to Egypt for education and support. One such person was Naser-e Khosrow (1002–ca.1077), who wrote a well-known book about his travels.

The Fatimid state experienced a crisis of succession following the death of its caliph-imam Mustansir in 1094, with some Isma'ilis claiming allegiance to his eldest son Abu Mansur Nizar and others to his younger son Abu'l Qasim Ahmad, known as Musta'ali. An Iranian Isma'ili by the name of Hasan-e Sabbah (d. 1124) became leader of the Nizari faction in Iran, where in 1090 he and a group of followers had captured a virtually impregnable castle called Alamut in the Alborz mountains. For the next two hundred years the Nizari Isma'ilis waged a guerrilla war against the Seljuk state, highlighted by spectacular public assassinations of important government figures.

Indeed, the word "assassin" derives from fantastic stories about this sect, transmitted to Europe by the Christian Crusaders in Palestine, claiming that the leader of the Nizari branch in Syria – the "Old Man of the Mountain," as they called him – would command the absolute obedience of his faithful by drugging them with hashish (hence *hashishiyyun* – "hashish-takers") in a wonderful garden full of beautiful women, meant to resemble paradise. According to popular legend, he would then send the young men out to perform their murderous tasks, promising a permanent return to paradise if they succeeded. Compelling as these stories may be, they are without any historical evidence to support them. In the Crusader stories the Syrian Nizaris became confounded with the Iranian branch, and in Marco Polo's colorful version the "Old Man of the Mountain" is the ruler of Alamut.

## Sufism in Iran

Mysticism, an approach found in all religions, can be characterized as an individual's quest for direct personal experience of the divine. The first Muslim mystics were perhaps those living in Syria and Egypt who were exposed to Christian monastic communities. But by the mid-eighth century a number of prominent mystics had appeared in the Iranian world as well. Though Sufi orders are found in all Muslim societies today (except in Saudi Arabia), the institutionalization of Sufi brotherhoods first took place predominantly in the Iranian east.

Many of the most important figures in classical Sufism were Iranians, including Hasan of Basra, Bayazid Bistami, Yahya ibn Muadh, Mohasebi, Sari al-Saqati, Jonayd, Mansur al-Hallaj, Qoshayri, Shehab al-din and Abu Najib Sohravardi, and many others. Itinerant Iranian Sufis were the major transmitters of Islam to India, China, and Southeast Asia – precisely, in other words, those parts of the world where most Muslims today reside.

Hasan Basri (d. 728) is one of the prominent founding figures of Muslim mysticism. He advocated an asceticism uncharacteristic of mainstream Islam, resisting the attachment to wealth and comfort that came as a corollary to Arab successes. Hasan's unworldliness expressed itself in an ethos of mourning, perhaps influenced by the popular Shi'ism of southern Iraq.

Abu Yazid, or Bayazid, of Bistam (d. 874) was an early proponent of what is often called "intoxicated" Sufism (*sukr*). His teachings on the mystical goal of ultimate "annihilation" (*fana'*) in the Divine may have drawn some influence from Indian ideas conveyed through his teacher, Abu Ali of Sindh. Bayazid used the story of the prophet Muhammad's miraculous night journey to heaven (*mi'raj*) as a model for the Sufi quest, a model which became very popular in later Sufism.

Mansur al-Hallaj (executed 922) is the paradigmatic example of the "intoxicated" approach. Sufi mystics had various ways of working themselves into ecstatic trances in which they came to feel a union with the divine. Some, the "sober" (*sahw*) Sufis, preferred to attain such states through practices such as mantra-like repetition of prayer formulas or the names of God (*dhikr* or *zekr*). Others, the "intoxicated" Sufis, might dance and whirl, sometimes accompanied by music and sometimes not. The mystics often tried to express the inexpressible through poetry, in many cases using the imagery of drunkenness and love as metaphors for the ecstatic experience. Such talk left them open to accusations of libertine behavior, which some Sufis felt was harmful to their cause.

One such "sober" Sufi was Jonayd of Baghdad (d. 910). Originally a teacher of Hallaj, Jonayd disowned his pupil's excessive public displays, such as dancing about and proclaiming "I am the Divine Truth!" Eventually Hallaj was executed for blasphemy – or, as some Sufis would have it, simply because he revealed the truth of mysticism which ordinary people were not yet prepared to hear.

By the tenth century clear rifts had developed not only between Sufis and non-Sufis but also among Sufis themselves. At the center of these tensions was the issue of authority and leadership; specifically, on what basis these should be derived. The legal scholars, who often served as advisors to government and played other important social roles, understandably felt that a lifetime of scholarship should serve as the primary basis for authority on religious matters. Sufi masters, more often than not, won followings largely through their personal charisma, though they were often well-studied in the formal religious sciences as well. Just as schools of Islamic law developed along lines laid down by certain founding figures, different mystical approaches became institutionalized as disciples of particular Sufi masters formalized and codified their teachings and practices.

The rift between Sufism and "orthodoxy" was healed somewhat by the great Iranian scholar Mohammad Ghazali (1058–1111), who has sometimes been called "the second greatest Muslim after Muhammad." Ghazali proved himself very early in life as a master of Islamic law in his capacity as professor at the prestigious Nezamiyyeh university in Baghdad. Following an intellectual and spiritual crisis in his thirties, however, Ghazali stepped down from his post and spent ten years exploring the Sufi path. On his return to teaching he developed an approach that reconciled legalism with mystical discipline, establishing the possibility at least that Sufism and Sunni orthodoxy could exist together.

Late in his life Ghazali also began to explore the metaphysics of light that had long been popular among Iranian Sufis. Shehab al-din Sohravardi (1153–1191) brought light mysticism to its fullest fruition, laying the foundation for a particularly Iranian philosophy he called *eshraqi* ("illuminationist"). Illuminationist philosophy, in which the symbols of light and darkness are applied to the Aristotelian notions of the "necessary" and the "contingent," reemerged later in Shi'ite form under the Safavids with the so-called school of Esfahan, culminating in the theosophy of Molla Sadra of Shiraz (d. 1640).

One of the great contributions of Iranian Sufis was in the realm of literature, especially poetry. No culture identifies with its poetic tradition more intensely than the Persian, and Sufis are among its most celebrated poets. None is better known and admired than Jalal al-din Rumi (1207–1273), whose loving devotion and ecstatic mysticism inspired the Turkish order that took his name – the Mevleviyya, after the honorific *mowlavi*, "my master" – a group known today as the whirling dervishes. Rumi's monumental work of rhymed couplets, the *Masnavi*, has been called "the Qur'an in Persian," so great is the impact of its message.

Other great Persian mystic poets include Sana'i, Attar, and Jami of Herat. Much Sufi poetry was didactic in nature, thus the Persian poetic tradition was a major vehicle for the spread of Islam, via Sufi masters, to Turkey, Central Asia, India, and China, where it served as the model for similar literatures in other languages.

With the conversion of Iran to Twelver Shi'ism in the sixteenth century two Shi'i Sufi orders became prominent, the Ne'matollahis and the Nurbakhshis. The Ne'matollahi order was founded by Nur al-din Ne'matollah b. 'Abdallah (1330–1431), who was born in Aleppo of Iranian parents but traced his genealogy to the fifth Shi'i Imam, Muhammad Baqir. He relocated to Central Asia but because of Tamerlane's pro-Sunni policies he later moved to Mahan in south-central Iran, near the city of Kerman. Unlike many Sufis who shunned worldly powers, but like the Sunni Naqshbandis in Central Asia, Nur al-din freely associated with the ruling class. As a result, the Ne'matollahi order has historically been popular among the Iranian upper classes.

The Nurbakhshis were an offshoot of the Kobravi order founded in Central Asia during the late thirteenth century by a saint named Najm al-din Kobra. A member of the Kobravi community in Khorasan, Mohammad ebn-e 'Abdallah (d. 1465), who was called "Nurbakhsh" ("giver of light"), gave this branch its distinctive Shi'i beliefs. The Ne'matollahi and the Nurbakhshi fraternities experienced their greatest growth under the Qajars in the nineteenth century. Both of these orders remain active in Iran today, although Sufism has been generally discouraged since the 1979 revolution.

## Twelver Shi'ism in Iran

In the late fourteenth century much of Iran was under the rule of a Turkic dynasty, the Aq Qoyunlu ("White Sheep" – a totemic clan name), based in Tabriz. The northwestern lands had long been a contest ground, alternately under the control of Iran and its western neighbor, first the Byzantine Romans and now the Ottoman Turks. The contiguous regions of western Azerbaijan and eastern Anatolia had been home since the eleventh century to various nomadic Turkic tribes who shunned any form of external authority.

The religiosity of the nomadic Turks was a hybrid of Islamic and their own pre-Islamic beliefs and practices. One prevalent tendency, however, was a focus on the person of Ali, the martyred nephew and son-in-law of Muhammad. At times the reverence for Ali approached deification. Some scholars have been quick to label any such "Ali-reverence" as Shi'ism, but given the clear lack of sophisticated theology among the tribes in question this identification is misleading. A better approach would be to say that such groups as the east Anatolian Turkish nomads displayed "shi'izing tendencies." The following poem exemplifies their unorthodox views about Ali:

> He opens the gate of Islam to the world.
> Know him to be God, do not call him human.
> He gives his miracles to the sons of Mary;
> he brings glad tidings to the sons of Adam.
> His mystery was together with God; he brought us into being
>     from non-existence.
> Through him the sanctuary [at Mecca] was ennobled to the
>     station of sainthood, the rank of nobility.
> He was God come down from heaven to earth to show him-
>     self to the creatures of the world.
> He intercedes for the universe; he stands to the Prophet as "your
>     flesh is my flesh."[2]

These popular conceptions are hard to reconcile with any mainstream Islamic tradition, in which no man is believed divine and Muhammad is the final prophet and ideal role model for Muslims.

In the late fifteenth century a Sunni Sufi order based in the town of Ardebil was growing increasingly militant. They were led by a family of shaykhs known as the Safavids, after their thirteenth-century ancestor Safi al-Din. As the Safavid family became politicized, they abandoned their original Sunni orientation and appealed to the "shi'izing tendencies" of nomadic groups throughout the region as a way of setting themselves up against the resented authority of the Sunni Ottomans. In 1501 an army of nomads under the leadership of the charismatic head of the Safavid family, a precocious fourteen-year-old by the name of Esma'il, dislodged the weak Aq Qoyunlu from Tabriz and declared their young guide the new Shah of Iran.

Esma'il's lack of familiarity with any kind of Islamic orthodoxy, whether Sunni or Shi'i, is clear from the content of the poems he composed to rally his troops. The above poem, which is attributed to him, indicates that the Safavid shaykhs had appropriated the heterodox beliefs of the rustic Turkish herdsmen they sought to mobilize. In the following example, young Esma'il shifts the focus of devotion to himself. Esma'il associates himself with all the most powerfully symbolic figures of Shi'ite legend, but hardly stops there:

> My name is Shah Esma'il. I am on God's side: I am the leader
>    of these warriors.
> My mother is Fatima, my father Ali:
> I too am one of the Twelve Imams.
> I took back my father's blood from Yazid [the Umayyad
>    Caliph who ordered his army against the martyr Husayn].
> Know for certain that I am the true coin of Haydar [i.e., Ali].
> Ever-living Khezr [prophet of eternal life], Jesus son of Mary,
> I am the Alexander of the people of this age.
> See Yazid, polytheist and accursed one,
> for I am free of the *qibla* of hypocrites.
> In my opinion prophecy is the innermost mystery of sainthood:
> I am a follower of Muhammad Mustafa.
> I have subjugated the world by the sword.
> I am Ali Murtida's Qanbar.
> My ancestor Safi, my father Haydar.
> I am a Ja'far of the people of bravery.
> I am a Husaynid, my curse upon Yazid.
> I am Khata'i, I am a servant of the king.[3]

It may certainly be questioned to what extent the views of Esma'il Safavi and his followers resembled any recognized form of Shi'ism. But once in power, the Safavids sought to identify themselves as a Shi'ite state, challenging the legitimacy of the Sunni Ottomans. Among the Iranian population of the time support for Shi'ism was not widespread, however. In fact, the Safavids could not find a single Shi'ite scholar anywhere in the country, and were forced to import clergy from Lebanon. One can only imagine the response of these Lebanese scholars, who were trained in the legal tradition of the sixth Shi'ite imam, Ja'far al-Sadiq, and followed the teachings of the Twelve Imams, once they were exposed to the bizarre religious beliefs of their new sponsors.

With the arrival in Iran of qualified Shi'ite jurists, however, any heterodoxy was quickly extinguished as the clerics were given free reign to impose Twelver Shi'ite law throughout the country. This change was not welcomed by Iran's Sunni majority, many of whom had to be converted by force, a process which lasted throughout the sixteenth century. From one town and village to the next, government agents saw to it that Iranians – including non-Muslims as well as Muslims – adopted Twelver practices, such as the cursing of the first three Caliphs (seen as usurpers of Ali's position) and the observation of the martyrdom of Husayn during the holy month of Muharram. Failure to do so resulted in persecution and often death.

By the end of the sixteenth century Iran had been reshaped into a Twelver Shi'ite nation, and it remains today the only officially Shi'ite state in the Muslim world. Throughout the Safavid period, which lasted until 1722, Shi'ite clergy exercised a powerful influence over Iranian politics and society. The eventual character of clerical influence in Iran was determined by an ideological struggle of the seventeenth century known as the *usuli-akhbari* conflict, described in the following chapter.

## Popular Shi'ite religiosity

In all societies there are occasional conflicts when religious authorities reject or attempt to suppress certain popular beliefs and practices they do not consider orthodox. At the beginning of the Safavid period the newly imported Shi'ite scholars were quick to put down the heterodox beliefs of the young king Esma'il and his tribal Turkic followers. This is an isolated example, however. Throughout the history of Shi'ism, the traditional ethos of mourning – which is focused first and foremost on the massacre of Muhammad's grandson Husayn at Karbala on the tenth day (*'ashura*) of the month of

Muharram in 680 CE – has often expressed itself in ways that many among the *'ulema'* found excessive.

The annual ten-day commemoration of this tragic event, which typically features mourning processions by chest-beating men and loud lamentations by women, has long been the most visible public expression of popular piety in Shi'ite societies. In environments where Shi'ites live side by side with Sunnis, as in India, the processions have sometimes been an occasion where intercommunal tensions flare up into violence. (The Shi'ite practice of cursing the first three "illegitimate" caliphs is often a trigger arousing Sunni hostility.) Although in overwhelmingly Shi'ite Iran this kind of tension is less prevalent, there too one sees occasional scuffles when rival processions converge.

More disturbing to many of the *'ulema'* is the practice of self-mutilation which has historically accompanied the Muharram processions. As in medieval Christianity and some other religious traditions, in Shi'ite Islam mourning rituals sometimes include rhythmic self-flagellations. One common form consists of throwing a chain repeatedly across one's back. Another, less common, has the devotee draw a knife blade across his own skull. For the most part Shi'ite religious scholars have condemned these practices, though the processions themselves are generally tolerated or even encouraged.

In Iran as part of the Muharram commemoration the events at Karbala have traditionally been reenacted in a form of popular theater called *ta'ziyeh*. Largely now confined to villages, the *ta'ziyeh* performances blur the line between actor and audience, and sometimes between fantasy and reality as on rare occasions when overwrought villagers have actually killed the person playing the role of Shimr, the "evil" general responsible for Husayn's death. (Needless to say, Shimr's role typically brings a higher fee for the actor.)

Another form of popular piety in Iran, which occurs throughout the year, is the making of pilgrimages to the shrines of revered historical figures. The most holy of these is the tomb of the eighth Shi'ite Imam, Reza (d. 818), in Mashhad (the name of the city itself means "place of the martyr," a reference to the fact that Reza, like all twelve Shi'ite Imams, is believed to have died of unnatural causes). Second in importance is the shrine of his sister Massumeh Fatemeh in the seminary city of Qom. Iranians flock to these two holy sites from all around the country. On a smaller scale, however, there are countless other shrines dedicated to the various descendants of the twelve Imams, called *imamzadeh*s, scattered throughout Iran. Important Sufi families have shrines as well. Such places are the frequent destinations of lesser pilgrimages, which may take the form of a weekend outing for a picnic and other kinds of family fun, effortlessly mixing piety and pleasure.

## The Persian garden as metaphor for paradise

The very word "paradise" is itself of Persian origin. Its modern Persian form, *ferdows*, means simultaneously "heaven" and "garden." (The corresponding Arabic term, *jannat*, has the same double meaning.) Both the English and modern Persian words are derived from the Old Persian *paira daeza*, meaning a walled enclosure, borrowed into ancient Greek as *paradaisos* and later into Arabic as *firdaws*.

One of the most pervasive yet subtle influences of Iranian culture throughout the world is the type of garden plan generally known as "Islamic." Such gardens are found not only throughout the Middle East, South Asia, and the rest of the Muslim world, but were also transmitted, via Spain, to much of the Western hemisphere. The basic design of an "Islamic" garden consists of a quadrangle, bisected (usually by channels of water) into quadrants, often with a pavilion or fountain in the middle, and with various plantings (consisting of trees, shrubs, flowers, and various groundcovers) throughout the quadrants. Such gardens are favored spots for picnics and lovers' trysts. The flowers, birds, and running water are all meant to evoke paradise.

In virtually all respects, however, this garden tradition is not "Islamic" as such, but has rather been Islamicized from the model of pre-Islamic Iran. Its precedents are very ancient: pottery bowls from as early as 4000 BCE show the familiar motifs of four quadrants with a pool at the center, the tree of life, and so on. By Sasanian times at the latest the garden quadrangle, called *chahar bagh* in Persian, had become the established design in Iran. A typical variant is the *hasht behesht*, or "eight paradises." The garden itself is often known as a *bustan*, literally "aromatic place," or *golestan*, "place of flowers," and figures as the setting for much of classical Persian poetry. The Persian garden is also one of the most common motifs in the design of Persian carpets, whose influence spread to South Asia, China, and Europe.

The heavenly gardens described in the Qur'an both recall and embellish the ancient Iranian garden model. In all there are 166 Qur'anic references to gardens. As with nature in general, gardens in the Qur'an are meant to be taken as signs (*ayat*) of God's divine order and perfection. In other words, the function of nature's beauty is to lead humans to God. From prehistoric times Iranians revered the natural world for its divine qualities, paying homage to the various *mainyu*s inhering in natural phenomena. For Muslim Iranians, this nature-reverence became sublimated to the level of symbolism, but remains nonetheless profound.

The fifty-fifth chapter of the Qur'an, entitled *al-Rahman* ("The Beneficent"), which describes the many beautiful gifts that God has bestowed on humans, contains the kind of rich imagery that evokes paradise in the minds of many Muslims. Verses 46–78 read as follows in the translation of Muhammad Marmaduke Pickthall:

> But for him who feareth the standing before his Lord there are two gardens.
> Which is it, of the favors of your Lord, that ye deny?
> Of spreading branches.
> Which is it, of the favors of your Lord, that ye deny?
> Wherein are two fountains flowing.
> Which is it, of the favors of your Lord, that ye deny?
> Wherein is every kind of fruit in pairs.
> Which is it, of the favors of your Lord, that ye deny?
> Reclining upon couches lined with silk brocade, the fruit of both the gardens near to hand.
> Which is it, of the favors of your Lord, that ye deny?
> Therein are those of modest gaze, whom neither man nor jinni will have touched before them.
> Which is it, of the favors of your Lord, that ye deny?
> (In beauty) like the jacynth and the coral-stone.
> Which is it, of the favors of your Lord, that ye deny?
> Is the reward of goodness aught save goodness?
> Which is it, of the favors of your Lord, that ye deny?
> And beside them are two other gardens,

Which is it, of the favors of your Lord, that ye deny?
Dark green with foliage.
Which is it, of the favors of your Lord, that ye deny?
Wherein are two abundant springs.
Which is it, of the favors of your Lord, that ye deny?
Wherein is fruit, the date-palm and pomegranate.
Which is it, of the favors of your Lord, that ye deny?
Wherein (are found) the good and beautiful –
Which is it, of the favors of your Lord, that ye deny?
Fair ones, close-guarded in pavilions –
Which is it, of the favors of your Lord, that ye deny?
Whom neither man nor jinni will have touched before them –
Which is it, of the favors of your Lord, that ye deny?
Reclining on green cushions and fair carpets.
Which is it, of the favors of your Lord, that ye deny?
Blessed be the name of thy Lord, Mighty and glorious!

Such a paradise garden has long been a major theme for poets, painters, and architects throughout the Persian-speaking world. One has only to think of the quatrains of Omar Khayyam, known to the English-speaking world through the versions of Edward Fitzgerald, or the Rose Garden of Sa'di or the lyric odes of Hafez and other classical poets. An inscription over the entryway to a Mughal palace in India reads, "If there is paradise on earth, it is here, it is here, it is here." Copies of the *Shah-nameh* and other popular works of literature are often embellished with miniature paintings which depict scenes reminiscent of the Qur'anic passage quoted above.

The nineteenth-century poet Fath Ali Khan of Kashan wrote the following verses in praise of a garden built at Tehran for his patron, the Qajar king Fath Ali Shah:

A name to be inscribed on the surface of heaven,
Still its height is loftier than the seven heavens,
And its extent is greater than the original eight paradises.
No wonder then that when Mani (the painter-prophet) and Azar
    (the father of Abraham, a professional idol-maker) saw its
    beautiful paintings,
They broke their brushes from shame.
. . .

The clear water of that pool is like the life-giving breath of Jesus,
And it seems that Mary may have washed her virgin-pure clothes in it.

. . .

I asked, "Is this the life-giving water?" and the answer came, "Yes."
I asked, "Is this garden paradise?" and wisdom replied, "Certainly."[4]

# 8

# THE BABI
# MOVEMENT
# AND THE
# BAHA'I FAITH

The eighteenth century in Iran was one of frequent turmoil. The country was shrinking dramatically in territory, successively losing control of Central Asia, Afghanistan, and western Kurdistan. (In the early nineteenth century the Caucasus provinces would be lost to Russia.) The activities of European businessmen, backed by increasingly powerful hegemonic states, weakened the Iranian economy and unsettled the Iranian merchant class, known as the *bazaari*s.

In 1722 the decadent Safavid regime fell to an army of Sunni Afghans. Authority over the workings of society was tenuously balanced between successive governments – the last Safavids, then the Afshars, then the Zand dynasty of Shiraz, and finally the Qajars from 1785 – and various religious leaders and their followings. Most powerful were the Shi'i *'ulema'*, the legal scholars, who had existed in a symbiotic relationship of mutual support and legitimation with the government throughout the Safavid period.

The ulema were loosely divided between those who derived law from a process of reasoning (*ejtehad* – the so-called *'usuli* clergy) and those who relied exclusively on the Qur'an, the hadiths, and the sayings of the Twelve Imams (the *akhbari*s). With the weakening and instability of government, however, came a resurgence of charismatic leadership from among the Sufi brotherhoods, particularly the Ne'matollahis and the Nurbakhshis whose esoteric teachings held sway over large numbers of the general population. At the same time, many Iranians continued to adhere more or less secretly to heterodox sects, especially in rural areas. One of the most significant of these was the Ahl-e Haqq in the Kurdish regions.

By the end of the eighteenth century many of the existing trends in Iranian religious thought had been synthesized in the so-called "Shaykhi" school of Shaykh Ahmad Ahsa'i (1756–1825), who drew his vision variously from illuminationist philosophy, Akhbari traditionism, and Isma'ili esotericism. The Shaykhi school was similar to Sufism in its focus on charismatic leadership, but differed in its teachings and use of sources. Significant numbers of the clergy became sympathetic to the Shaykhi approach, which privileged the special insight of the movement's leader over Usuli-type legalism. The Usuli class, in response, sought to discredit the Shaykhis (and the Sufis, for that matter) as charlatans.

Among its many innovations, the Shaykhi eschatology proposed a radical interpretation of the Islamic notion of resurrection. Ahsa'i taught that after death the body perishes, while the soul goes to a purificatory realm called the *barzakh* (bridge), ultimately to be reunited with its original celestial body, cleansed of all earthly tarnish. However, those possessing transcendent insight (that is, dreams and visions), could reach an intermediate zone between heaven and earth, called Hurqalya, while still alive. Transcendence to the intermediary world of Hurqalya would give access to the guidance of the Hidden Imam. Shaykh Ahsa'i himself, naturally, was considered by his followers to possess this ability, and thus to have privileged access to the authoritative teaching of the Hidden Imam.

Considered by his disciples to be "the Perfect Shi'ite" – a notion dating back to the Sixth Imam, Ja'far, and similar in some ways to the "Perfect Man" of the Sufis – Shaykh Ahsa'i was seen as the "gate" (*bab*) between the earthly sphere and the visionary world of the Imam. As such, Shaykh Ahsa'i could claim a more direct authority in Twelver Shi'ite society than that of the legal scholars, whose connections with the Hidden Imam relied on chains of transmission more than a thousand years old. The fact that a millennium had now passed since the occultation of the Twelfth Imam heightened expectations of his return. Messianic speculations were rife among many Iranian Shi'ite sects of the time, including the followers of Shaykh Ahsa'i. Twelver Shi'ism taught that the return of the Hidden Imam as the Mahdi (messiah) would herald the final victory over the forces of evil, the restoration of true Shi'ism, and ultimately the Resurrection and the Day of Judgment. A fervent longing for this event was central to the Twelver Shi'ite ethos.

While government officials occasionally sought support from charismatic spiritual leaders, on the whole they preferred to ally themselves with the Usuli scholars. As the rationalist Usuli faction were increasingly able to marginalize the traditionist Akhbari jurists, they came to see Sufi and Shaykhi teachers as their main rivals for authority. Their attempts to delegitimize and crush the latter escalated throughout the early Qajar period, culminating in the violent, government-supported repression of the recently emerged Babi movement in the 1840s.

## The Babi movement

The Qajar regime was characterized throughout its century-and-a-half of rule by its general weakness, unpopularity, and insecurity in the face of numerous domestic and external threats. Arguably the greatest internal disruption in nineteenth-century Iran was a short-lived but, for the Qajars, highly traumatic challenge known as the Babi movement which lasted from 1844 until 1852.

The focus of this challenge to the powers that be – that is, the intertwined temporal authority of the Qajar elites and the spiritual authority of the Usuli ulema – was a prophetic figure by the name of Seyyed Ali Mohammad, a young merchant of Shiraz, known to his followers as the Bab. As we have seen, the notion of one special person serving as "gate" (*bab*) to the Hidden Imam had a long history in Twelver Shi'ism, but claims about the status of Seyyed Ali Mohammad did not end there. Eventually he would say he was the promised Mahdi himself, and abrogate Islam altogether in calling for passage into a new era.

Seyyed Ali Mohammad was born in 1819 into a bazaari family, and showed a strong interest in religion from an early age. At twenty he traveled to the holy Shi'ite city of Karbala in Iraq (the site of Imam Husayn's martyrdom in 680), where he made the acquaintance of local Shaykhis and attended classes held by Shaykh Ahsa'i's successor, Seyyed Kazem of Rasht. Many of the Shaykhis (including Seyyed Kazem himself) were deeply impressed by the piety and insight of the young merchant. After a year or less he returned to Shiraz, but when Seyyed Kazem died in 1844 without designating a successor a number of important Shaykhis eventually came to believe that Seyyed Ali Mohammad, despite his lack of formal legal training, was the new *bab*, the one person alive with direct access to the Hidden Imam. The timing was significant: by 1844 it had been one thousand lunar years since the disappearance of the Twelfth Imam.

The Bab soon intimated to his disciples that his status was greater than that of his predecessors. His teachings, which he began to write down as sacred books, constituted nothing less than divine revelation. (Orthodox Muslims believed there would be no revelation subsequent to the Qur'an, and that Muhammad had been the "Seal of the Prophets.") The Bab and his followers spread the word throughout Iran and the Shi'ite cities of Iraq that the return of the Twelfth Imam as the promised Mahdi was imminent. They staged an abortive rally in Karbala in 1845 on behalf of the hoped-for Mahdi, and later the same year the Bab was briefly arrested for blasphemy in his home town of Shiraz. Apparently among his closer disciples the Bab had begun to claim that in fact he himself was the long-awaited one.

In Twelver Shi'ite society such a claim had enormous implications. In the absence of the Hidden Imam, believers were taught to accommodate themselves to the temporal powers that be, and follow the guidance of the ulema who were acting as the Imam's vice-regents. With the return of the Imam, both the existing secular and spiritual authorities would become obsolete. It comes as little surprise that as the Bab's following grew, his movement was met with harsh repression from the Usuli clergy who began to issue *fatwa*s (legal opinions) to the effect that the Bab was an apostate and thus eligible for the death penalty. The Qajar government was somewhat slower to perceive the threat, at first seeing the Bab as simply mentally unbalanced.

In the summer of 1848, however, the authorities acceded to the ulema's demands that the Bab be arrested once again, and he was tried in Tabriz for blasphemy. During the course of this trial the Bab made public his claim that he was the Mahdi. In the wake of the Bab's trial Babi missionaries throughout Iran were increasingly harassed and beaten by the public, egged on by the ulema.

Although a large proportion of the Bab's early disciples came from within the Shaykhi movement, many prominent Shaykhis rejected his claims and began to write refutations of his teachings. The Bab responded by branding his leading Shaykhi opponent as the "Tree of Negation" and the "Embodiment of Hell-Fire." Meanwhile, a remarkable Iranian woman by the name of Fatemeh Begum Baraghani (1814–1852), who is better known as Qorrat al-'Ayn ("Solace of the Eyes" – a title she had received from Seyyed Kazem) had become the leading champion of the Bab's cause in the holy city of Karbala. Her fervent support of the Bab polarized the Shaykhi community of Iraq. In 1847 Qorrat al-'Ayn was deported by Iraq's Ottoman rulers and returned to Iran where she pursued her activities. Babi missionaries continued to win converts, largely through tapping into existing networks of Shaykhi clergy and members of the merchant class (the *bazaari*s) with whom they had close ties.

During the summer of 1848 while the Bab was undergoing his trial and imprisonment in Azerbaijan, a large group of his followers gathered in a village called Badasht in northern Iran to discuss how he might be liberated. Qorrat al-'Ayn spoke at the meeting and shocked the audience by removing her veil. Though some contemporary commentators have seen this as a feminist gesture, more likely it was meant to symbolize the Bab's abrogation of Islamic law. In any case the Badasht event brought together some of the most radical elements from within the Babi movement, and raised the concern of the government and the ulema alike. Although it is impossible to know how many Iranians were followers of the Bab, they may have numbered as many as 100,000 – perhaps two-and-a-half percent of the country's settled population. It was no longer possible for the powers that be to take this movement lightly.

In the wake of the Bab's trial and the conference at Badasht, the revolutionary fervor of some Babis was such that they began a march from Mashhad in eastern Iran, aiming to reach Azerbaijan and free the Bab so that his mission might be fulfilled. They were halted by a mob along the way, however, and after a brief skirmish the Babis took refuge in a shrine (dedicated to one Shaykh Tabarsi and named after him). They fortified the shrine and holed up for a seven-month siege until they were finally tricked into surrender and then massacred. The Tabarsi incident established once and for all the conviction in the minds of the Qajar elite that the Babis were a dangerous insurrectionary movement and not to be tolerated.

Over the next year-and-a-half groups of Babis engaged in armed struggle against the establishment in several parts of the country, most notably in the towns of Yazd, Zanjan, and Nayriz. Finally the government ordered the execution of the Bab, hoping to end the uprisings. In July 1850 the Bab was brought before a firing squad in Tabriz. After the dust cleared from the first volley, the Bab and a condemned companion were seen to have vanished. They turned up after a quick search of the premises – the shots had missed and severed the ropes which held them – and they were then definitively executed. But it would take another two years for the Qajar government to crush the movement once and for all.

With their leader gone, the disorganized remnants of the Bab's followers began to look for the successor he had promised, "he whom God will make manifest." Among at least twenty-five Babis who came forward to claim this identity, two brothers emerged: Mirza Yahya Nuri (1831–1912), known as Sobh-e Azal ("Morning of Eternity") and Mirza Hossein Ali Nuri (1817–1892), called Baha'u'llah ("Glory of God"). However, after a botched attempt to assassinate the Qajar ruler Naser al-Din Shah in 1852, for which the Babis were blamed and thus subjected to still harsher reprisals, the movement went largely underground. Most of their leaders, including Qorrat al-'Ayn, had been killed. Those Babis who survived adopted the age-old Shi'ite practice of *taqiyya*, dissimulation of one's true beliefs to ensure the survival of the religious community.

## Babi beliefs

The teachings of the Bab offered radical reinterpretations of familiar Iranian and Islamic religious notions. As in mainstream Islam he taught that revelation was progressive, but contrary to the orthodox Islamic notion of Muhammad's prophecy as being the final culmination of all previous prophecies, the Bab argued that divine inspiration is ongoing and comes in different guises to meet the needs of different ages. The heart of the Bab's revelations, which were expressed both in Arabic and in Persian, were contained in holy books called the *Qayyum al-Asma'* ("The Resurrection of [Holy] Names") and the *Bayan* ("The Exposition"). All in all the Bab claimed to have received half a million verses of revelation.

In Babi thought the concept of resurrection (*qiyamat*), understood in Zoroastrianism and Islam to be something that will occur after death, was revised to mean something that had begun on earth with the Bab's revelation. Salvation – perceived as inclusion in a "community of light" – would be attained by recognizing the Bab as God's messenger and working to disseminate his message. Redemption was thus an ongoing process undertaken by the individual, rather than a single cosmic future event. The temporal authority of the Twelver Shi'ite clergy, based as it was on their claim to represent the Hidden Imam until his eventual reappearance, was rendered obsolete.

Though the Bab eventually called for the abrogation of Islamic law, at first he taught his followers to adhere to the *shari'a*, with some additional practices such as a three-month fast and special prayers. (He also enjoined them to abstain from smoking.) After his imprisonment and declaration of Mahdihood, however, the Bab replaced the *shari'a* with a new set of laws which were contained in the *Bayan*. Ritual prayers were subordinated to individual ones, and the emphasis on ritual purity – which was nothing less than an obsession in legalistic Shi'ism – was superseded by spiritual purity. The obligatory pilgrimage to Mecca was replaced by a pilgrimage to the Bab's home in Shiraz. The traditional Shi'ite notions of martyrdom and holy war were reinterpreted in Babi terms.

The Bab furthermore called his followers to avoid mixing or intermarrying with non-Babis, and to shun non-Babi books and learning. He discouraged polygamy and made divorce more difficult. In business dealings, he allowed the charging of interest (forbidden under the *shari'a*), and he established a new calendar based on cycles of 19. The Bab promulgated a system of occultic protections, requiring his followers to make and carry special talismans. Babis were to eschew the color black, even writing with black ink, as this color was associated with the Abbasids who had persecuted the Shi'i Imams.

The new world envisioned by the Bab did not come about, and the efforts of his followers to create it ended in bloody tragedy. In light of the Bab's failure to establish a new set of norms in Iranian society, perhaps the greatest legacy of his teaching is his doctrine of expecting "he whom God will make manifest," setting the stage for a subsequent prophet even greater than himself. In the minds of a majority of surviving Babis, that figure was soon to emerge.

## The emergence of the Baha'i faith

The Nuri brothers were, somewhat atypically among followers of the Bab, from a noble landowning family with ties to the Qajar government. Their social status may have played a role in earning them the respect of their fellow Babis, and also perhaps helped protect them from government reprisals during the persecutions of 1848–1852. (At the height of the Babi disruptions the Qajar Prime Minister, Amir Kabir, actually offered Mirza Hossein Ali a government position in hopes of co-opting his influence.) Though information on the Babis in the years following the crushing of the movement is scarce, it appears that Mirza Yahya had the largest following among the many contenders for leadership. Indeed it was widely considered that the Bab himself had appointed him as his successor, though it is also possible that this was merely a diversionary move to protect the true designate, Mirza Yahya's elder half-brother Mirza Hossein Ali.

During this obscure time the movement seems to have split between followers of Sobh-e Azal (that is, Mirza Yahya) and those of Baha'u'llah (Mirza Hossein Ali). Baha'u'llah was exiled to Iraq, where Sobh-e Azal also moved but kept a low profile, while Baha'u'llah assumed a more public role of teaching and leadership. Tensions arose between the two as Baha'u'llah increasingly became the focus of attention for Babi devotees. By 1866, when Baha'u'llah formally advanced the claim that he was the one "whom God shall make manifest," his supporters were by far the majority. The smaller Azali faction remained ideologically close to the original Babi teachings, whereas Baha'u'llah's approach had changed dramatically.

Like the Bab, Baha'u'llah was incredibly prolific in his writings. It was said that he received as many as one thousand verses of revelation in an hour. Many of his works, such as the *Ode to the Dove* and the *Seven Valleys* were Sufi-sounding and ecstatic in nature, describing his own religious experiences in heavily symbolic language, while others, like the *Book of Certitude* and *Hidden Words*, were instructive or explained the hidden meanings of things (such as specific words or letters) in the usual esoteric tradition.

Perhaps the most significant departure from the Babi precedent was Baha'u'llah's rejection of militancy. His quietistic approach combined with his increasing popularity led some in both the

Ottoman and Qajar governments to feel it would be worthwhile to cultivate positive relations with him and his followers. Baha'u'llah, however, resisted any politicization of his movement. Even so, his charismatic appeal and growing following brought hostility from the ulema who saw their own monopoly on religious authority once again being threatened. In 1863, at the instigation of some Iranian opponents, Baha'u'llah was removed from Baghdad by the Ottomans and transferred to the capital, Istanbul. Surrounded by an adoring entourage of devotees, Baha'u'llah offended Ottoman officials by refusing to associate with them, which led to a second exile to Edirne (Adrianople) on the western border of the empire.

The activities of Baha'u'llah's followers in Edirne (which likely included attempts to convert local Muslims) and the constant coming and going of pilgrims from Iran did nothing to ease the discomfort of the Ottoman authorities. In 1868 they relocated him once again, this time to the decrepit port of Akka (Acre) on the Mediterranean coast of Palestine, where he spent the rest of his life. He died in 1892, and his shrine there contains a beautiful garden in the Persian style which is maintained to this day by Baha'i volunteers from around the world.

## Baha'u'llah's teachings

As in Shaykhi and Babi teaching, the Baha'i belief system posits a remote, unknowable God who can be accessed only through the medium of his human manifestations. Baha'u'llah was believed by his followers to be merely the most recent in a succession of divine manifestations which included Zoroaster, Abraham, Moses, Jesus, Muhammad, and the Bab, among others. Following a transformative rather than a strictly linear cosmology, Baha'is fully expect that other such manifestations will continue to appear in the future. Baha'u'llah had a great respect for Christianity and the Bible, which he quoted often in his own writings. Just as he claimed to be the one "whom God will make manifest" to the Babis, to Christians he implied that he represented the awaited return of Christ.

The immediate millenarian impulse in Shaykhi and Babi thought was refocused in the Baha'i faith to a more distant future, the goal of restoring society through the rule of the Imam being replaced with the notion of a "Most Great Peace." Whereas the former movements had focused on the Shi'ite world of Iran, Baha'u'llah's vision encompassed the entire world. All humans, Baha'u'llah taught, are of the same essence and substance. The world, in his view, was "but one country, and mankind its citizens." As he put it to the English Iranianist E. G. Browne:

> That all nations should become one in faith and all men as brothers; that the bonds of affection and unity between the sons of men should be strengthened; that diversity of religion should cease, and differences of race be annulled – what harm is there in this? . . . Yet so it shall be; these fruitless strifes, these ruinous wars shall pass away, and the "Most Great Peace" shall come . . . Do not you in Europe need this also? Is not this that which Christ foretold? . . . Yet do we see your kings and rulers lavishing their treasures more freely on means for the destruction of the human race than on that which would conduce to the happiness of mankind . . . These strifes and this bloodshed and discord must cease, and all men be as one kindred and one family . . . Let not a man glory in this, that he loves his country; let him rather glory in this, that he loves his kind.[1]

As a step toward fulfilling this universalist vision, Baha'u'llah wrote letters to various world leaders (including the Ottoman Sultan, the Shah of Iran, the Tsar of Russia, and the Queen of England, among others) urging them to meet and set down rules for negotiation among what is called today "the international community." In fact, the details of Baha'u'llah's proposal bear a remarkable resemblance to what would come into being in the mid-twentieth century as the United Nations. Interestingly, however, in his writings Baha'u'llah does not challenge the institution of monarchy as such; indeed, he idealizes it in the ancient Iranian terms of the king as "Shadow of God on Earth."

Another radical feature of Baha'i teaching, anticipated perhaps in Babism, was a reduction in gender inequality that was highly dramatic in the context of patriarchal Iranian society. To some extent this may have been an echo of women's emancipatory movements in Europe, which were reported by Iranian travelers and in the Iranian media which were read by the literate classes. Many aristocratic and even royal Iranian women, though most often housebound, engaged in written correspondence with Baha'u'llah. In his *Most Holy Book* (*Ketab-e aqdas*), Baha'u'llah called for the education of girls as well as boys, and urged monogamous marriages. Elsewhere he wrote that "the Servants of God and His handmaidens are regarded as on the same plane,"[2] and "Verily, in the eyes of Baha women are the same as men. All are God's creation, which He created in his likeness, that is, they are manifestations of his names and attributes."[3] Baha'u'llah suggests that future prophets ("manifestations of God," in Baha'i terms) could be female:

> Know thou moreover that in the Day of Revelation were He to pronounce one of the [female believers] to be the manifestation of all His excellent titles, unto no one is given the right to utter why or wherefore, and should one do so he would be regarded as an unbeliever in God and numbered with such as have repudiated His truth.[4]

Elsewhere, however, Baha'u'llah maintained a degree of gender imbalance. One example is in his treatment of inheritance law. Clearly the reversal of centuries of patriarchy would not occur overnight, but there is a distinct trend in this direction throughout the subsequent development of Baha'i thought.

Baha'u'llah taught that the primary earthly task of all Baha'is was to work towards the Most Great Peace. Since this could only be done by actively participating in society, asceticism was shunned. Begging was likewise forbidden, as was giving to beggars. (The needs of poor Baha'is would be taken care of through donations to the House of Justice, the central Baha'i institution.) In a radical departure from the revolutionary politics of the Babis, Baha'is were urged to remain loyal to whatever government they lived under. They were to obey the laws of their society, and associate freely with people of all races and religions. In place of martyrdom, Baha'is were to spread the faith through missionary work.

## The Baha'i community in Iran and beyond

With an established center and charismatic leader (albeit existing outside Iran) during the latter part of the nineteenth century, the Baha'i mission in Iran brought large numbers of converts into the fold. Christian missionaries from Europe, who were becoming active in

Iran at the same time, regularly noted the rapid spread of the Baha'i faith. Some even speculated that it would one day displace Islam as Iran's official religion. Predictably, however, Baha'i successes brought a backlash from the country's established Shi'ite clergy, and persecutions once again began to rise, especially in Esfahan. Overall, however, Baha'is could feel their fortunes were improving, especially since they were gaining influential sympathizers in government and business. Among the educated and affluent classes of Iran, the numbers of Baha'is were disproportionately high.

Baha'u'llah's son and eventual successor, 'Abdu'l-Baha (1844–1921), set up an infrastructure for the growing Baha'i communities worldwide. This included the establishment of national "spiritual assemblies" and the founding of Baha'i schools, in Iran and in other nations where Baha'is lived. During this period many Iranian Baha'is traveled to other countries as missionaries. Often, as in Egypt, Turkey, Russian-held Central Asia, British India, and Burma, they succeeded in converting significant numbers from among expatriate Iranian merchant communities. The most thriving Baha'i community was that of Ashkhabad (in what is now Turkmenistan), which became the site of the first Baha'i House of Worship.

The Baha'i faith was brought to the United States by an Egyptian convert named Ibrahim George Kheiralla in 1894. Establishing himself in Chicago, by 1900 Kheiralla had won some 2000 American converts. After a rupture between Kheiralla and 'Abdu'l-Baha in Akka, most American Baha'is gave their allegiance to the latter, who personally visited the United States in 1912. American Baha'is launched missionary efforts to Europe and the Pacific, and before long Baha'i could no longer be considered primarily an Iranian religion.

Baha'i beliefs and social organization were institutionalized under the leadership of 'Abdu'l-Baha's Oxford-educated grandson, Shoghi Effendi (1897–1957). The Baha'i faith today claims upwards of five million adherents of all races and cultural backgrounds, and Baha'i Houses of Worship have been built in every continent except Antarctica. Having no clergy, Baha'i communities function on three levels of elected representation: local, national, and through the Universal House of Justice, which is located in Haifa, Israel.

In Iran Baha'is maintained their existence as the country's largest non-Muslim community throughout the late Qajar and Pahlavi periods up to the revolution of 1979. Under Mohammad Reza Shah, who was installed on the throne by the British after they exiled Reza Shah to South Africa in 1941, Iran's Baha'is were tolerated by the government but were often harassed by fanatical Shi'ite elements such as the Feda'iyin-e Eslam. Under pressure from the ulema, in 1955 Baha'is were subjected to pogroms. During the 1960s and 1970s their situation improved, as Baha'is found their way into important positions in industry and academia. Muslims accused the Pahlavi government of exercising favoritism towards the Baha'is, but more likely Baha'i successes were due to an emphasis on education which made them candidates for the kinds of position that were opening up through the Shah's rapid modernization program.

Yet while the Baha'i community in much of the world has increased steadily since the beginning of the twentieth century, in Iran as in other Muslim countries their numbers have remained static or declined. Presumably the Islamic ban on apostasy has played some role in this, as well as prejudice stemming from the Baha'i faith's origins in an Islamic cultural context. (All Baha'i activities were banned in Egypt in 1960 and in Iraq in 1970.) With the advent of an Islamic government from 1979 onwards, persecution of Baha'is once again became a matter of official policy.

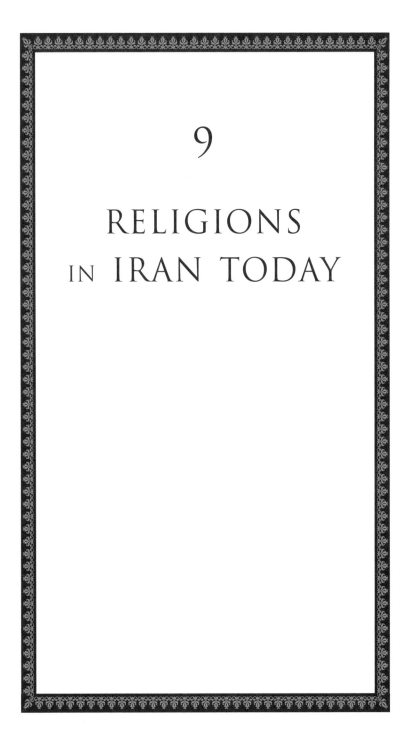

9

# RELIGIONS
## IN IRAN TODAY

In 1979 Iranians overthrew their 2500-year-old tradition of monarchy – the oldest in the world at that time (albeit with occasional interruptions). Iranians themselves were probably more surprised than anyone at this remarkable turn of events. They had always, throughout their long history, been under the rule of an autocratic government, apart from a brief two-year experiment with democracy from 1951–1953 which was overthrown in a CIA-sponsored coup. (The popularly elected regime of Mohammad Mosaddeq was too independent-minded for the British and American governments of the time to accept, especially after he nationalized Iran's oil industry.)

Although a broad-based opposition had been taking shape throughout the 1970s in response to the policies of Shah Mohammad Reza Pahlavi, few Iranians imagined that the monarchy, buttressed as it was by a US-supplied Iranian army, could ever fall to popular pressure. But the Shah, enfeebled by cancer and increasingly unable to respond to growing mass demonstrations, fled the country in December 1978. On 1 February 1979, the country rallied around the return from exile of Ruhollah Khomeini, a Shiʻite scholar of the highest level – Ayatollah, literally, "Sign of God" – who became the spiritual leader of the modern world's first Islamic revolution.

Clerical ranks in Twelver Shiʻism are determined by one's peers. While Khomeini had received the highest form of recognition from his fellow legal scholars, he was not generally considered to be the most highly qualified of his rank.[1] He was, however, the most outspoken, beginning with his protests against the Shah's modernization policies in 1963 which led to his arrest and eventual exile the following year. From the Shi'ite holy city of Najaf in Iraq he continued to speak out against the Iranian regime, and his speeches were widely circulated in Iran via cassette tapes. Since Khomeini was able and willing to say what many Iranians felt in their hearts but feared to express, he acquired a special authority, particularly among the growing masses of urban poor, who were mostly displaced peasants unable to find work in the cities. Such people tended to congregate in neighborhood mosques, where Khomeini's tapes were often played.

Khomeini was not the only major Iranian figure to play a role in mobilizing religious discourse in opposition to the Shah's government. Beginning in the 1960s Mehdi Bazargan, a French-trained engineer, spoke out against the Shah's marginalizing of traditional Iranian religious values, arguing that Islam and modernization were not incompatible. In the 1970s another non-clerical intellectual, Ali Shariati, won many Iranians over to his personal vision of Islamic modernism, especially university students. Religious ideology was also used by Iran's two major anti-government guerrilla groups, the Feda'iyin-e Eslam, founded in 1946, and the Mojahedin-e Khalq, established in 1965. So by the late 1970s much of the revolutionary impulse in Iran had a religious flavor.

And yet, during the years leading up to the revolution the range of opposition groups in Iran had run the full political spectrum, from the communist Tudeh party to French-inspired secular intellectuals urging a European-style democracy. How the most extreme branch of religious radicals, the Hezbollah or "Party of God," came so quickly to seize the reins of power uniquely for themselves is a complex question which continues to be hotly debated and discussed by political scientists and historians. But a simple explanation would be that among all the diverse political groups vying for a voice in the new, post-monarchical government, many apart from the religious extremists agreed on one thing: that no particular voice (except that of the monarchists) should be excluded. By an irony which was perhaps nevertheless inevitable, the religious radicals, who were decidedly a minority, were able to silence the others who did not take it upon themselves to silence them first.

The ironies do not end there. Many of the leading religious scholars of Iran – that is, Khomeini's peers – refused to take a leadership role in the new government, on the basis that to do so would be in violation of Shi'ite principles. Since long-established Shi'ite political theory argued that all worldly government in the absence of the Twelfth Imam was illegitimate, even an "Islamic" government was disallowed until such time as the Imam's promised return. Yet among the masses more familiar with dramatic symbols than with the finer points of Shi'ite thought, this doctrine was altered to meet the needs of those who would seize power. When "Imam" Khomeini's plane arrived in Tehran from Paris on that fateful day in 1979, Iranian newspapers ran the banner headline: "The Imam Has Returned." Since that time, the age-old term took on a new reference, and in popular parlance "the Imam" was henceforth understood to mean not the promised Mahdi but rather the Ayatollah Khomeini.

Since many of those most qualified to serve in a Shi'ite theocracy chose not to do so, the field was left open to those less bound by their knowledge of Shi'ite law. The first parliaments of the newly declared Islamic Republic of Iran were notorious for their inclusion of semi-literate preachers (*mollas*) from the villages, who brought their parochial perspectives and often bigoted attitudes to the project of drawing up a whole new social and legal system. Against this back-drop of political disarray Iran was suffering the usual catastrophic corollaries to revolution, such as a breakdown in public security, frequent mob rule, looting, and the carrying out of mass executions by ad hoc kangaroo courts. In September 1980 Iran's neighbor Saddam Hussein of Iraq, fearing the mollas' stated aims to export their revolution, compounded the chaos by invading the country.

The Iraqi despot, claiming sovereignty over the contested Shatt al-Arab River separating the two countries, was motivated both by the Iranian radicals' threats to export their revolution to Iraq's Shi'ite majority (Saddam's government being dominated by Sunnis) and by the hope that a country already in disorder would quickly fall to his better-armed forces. In the event, however, the emergence of an outside threat galvanized the Iranian people behind their new leadership. It may well be that contrary to the aims of Saddam and the US intelligence services which supported him at the time, the Iraqi invasion actually strengthened a revolutionary regime that might not otherwise have survived.

Indeed throughout the Iran-Iraq conflict, which lasted until 1988, the Iranian government was able to distract public attention from its own failed policies by citing the urgencies of war. Once that distraction was removed, and especially with the loss of a charismatic authority figure upon the death of Khomeini in 1989, economically challenged Iranians began to question the regime and hold it accountable for the country's worsening conditions. What began as private murmurs in the late 1980s had erupted by 1997 in a surprising national election in which more than three-quarters of the vote went to a soft-spoken intellectual reformer, Mohammad Khatami, a former Minister of Islamic Guidance who had been banished by the previous government to a library job for being "too liberal" in enforcing the government's censorship of literature and film. The same elections swept most of the religious clerics from parliament, replacing them in many cases with people who held Ph.D.'s from American or European universities.

The 2001 elections, which retained Khatami as president and confirmed the trend in parliament, showed that Iranians had overwhelmingly rejected the excesses and restrictions of a theocratic government. Khatami, himself a cleric but who cites French philosophers as often as he does the Qur'an, has stated repeatedly his view that "if religion comes into conflict with freedom, then religion will suffer."[2] Iranian attitudes after more than two decades of Islamic revolution confirm the predictive value of these words. One of the ironies of present-day Iran is that while formally all government-approved initiatives in the country must be justified in Islamic terms, government officials now admit that "if you want to win popular support for a program in Iran today, it is best to leave Islam out of it."[3]

While Iran is still far from constituting a model of democracy (candidates are screened by an unelected council of religious leaders, for example), the past two cycles of national elections have demonstrated a democratic process that excels in certain respects those seen in some Western societies. In contrast to the situation in the United States, for example, recent Iranian elections have expressed the real desires of the popular majority, rather than merely those of plutocratic industrial interests or of a "least worst" mentality. No American election has ever approached the more than seventy percent voter turnout seen in Iran, where the right to vote is exercised enthusiastically for the most part and without the coercion often present in other developing countries.

And yet Iran continues to flounder in its domestic policies, with political arrests and other human rights violations regularly on-going. This, of course, is the narrow reality that gets reported in the international press. In a speech in 2001 US president George W. Bush included Iran in what he called an "axis of evil," along with erst-while ally Iraq and perennial pariah-state North Korea. Chief among Iran's cited sins were its nuclear program – despite the fact that US ally Pakistan had acquired nuclear weapons with impunity, and even sold the technology to North Korea – and Iran's support of Palestinian "terrorist organizations," the obvious similarities with US support for the Nicaraguan contras and many other such groups remaining unacknowledged.[4]

If Iran's experiment with theocracy increasingly appears to have lost its popular support, why does the country still retain the appearance and general apparatus of an Islamic state? The main rea-son would seem to be the fossilized presence of a clause in the 1980 constitution, which provides for the *velayat-e faqih*, the "Rule of the Supreme Jurist," an unelected office tailor-made for Khomeini. The judiciary, the army, and the police are all under the ultimate author-ity of this office, which has been held since Khomeini's death by the uncharismatic and reactionary Ayatollah Ali Khamene'i. Thus, under Iran's present system, while the executive and legislative branches of government are democratically elected, the judiciary branch is not, and for the last several years the country has been stymied by an ongoing struggle between the first two bodies of government against the recalcitrant third. At this point the future of the Islamic Republic is unclear, but it is hard to imagine its disappearance as long as the office of *velayat-e faqih* survives in the country's constitution.

## Religious thought in an Islamic state

The elevation of religion from an oppositional force under Shah Mohammad Reza Pahlavi to official ideology under the Islamic Republic placed a new set of burdens upon Iran's religious thinkers. While formerly they could merely criticize, now they were held responsible for the welfare of Iranians. At first the instabilities caused by revolution and war constrained the parameters of religious discussion, and an appropriate governing orthodoxy was urgently sought. But as the theocratic state became established throughout the 1980s, a widening array of perspectives sought to express themselves within the required Islamic framework, pushing the boundaries in many directions.

One major aspect of the evolving religious discussion centered on gender roles, particularly the status of women. Although early on in the revolution women were purged from many positions and Islamic covering (*hejab*) was enforced upon all females over the age of nine, the social conditions of the 1980s could not prevent women from entering or reentering the public sphere in nearly every field, a process which has been accelerating ever since. With an entire generation of boys and young men involved in the war effort against Iraq, women came to the workforce in ever-increasing numbers and in virtually all professions. The economic and professional empowerment of Iranian women was debated and largely justified through ongoing discussions among religious scholars, particularly the *hawzeh* (religious circle) of the seminaries of Qom.

Another important area of discussion was politics, especially the proper role of an Islamic government. The Islamic Republic, for all its appeal to tradition, was in fact a tremendously radical undertaking. Nothing like an "Islamic" democracy (in the modern sense of "democracy") had ever been tried in the world before, and some wondered if the notion could really even exist. And yet it must be said that since the late 1990s Iran has initiated a kind of democratic process while retaining an underpinning of traditional Islamic values.

Not that this success has been complete in either respect. Iranians do vote in elections – although some, frustrated with the process, are now boycotting them – and they now generally get their preferred candidates. Still, personal freedoms remain severely compromised in many ways, and any number of words or deeds can land one in jail. Young Iranians especially are increasingly impatient with the slow pace of reform, as attested in massive street demonstrations by students and others during the summer of 2003. And while it continues to be the case that any officially sanctioned undertaking must be justified in Islamic language, for many Iranians this language has become nothing more than a veneer.

Since the 1980s, moreover, the struggle over who speaks for Shi'i Islam has intensified. The traditional monopoly on religious authority held by the ulema has been challenged by figures such as Abdol Karim Soroush and Mohsen Kadivar. Soroush, whom Western journalists like to call "the Martin Luther of Islam," has acquired an enormous following among religiously minded intellectuals, especially of the younger generation. Frequent attempts by groups of reactionary thugs to disrupt his public lectures have not diminished his popularity, though he occasionally takes refuge abroad (Harvard University in the United States being a favored getaway). In essence Soroush's message is that Islam should not remain static, a relic of past conditions. He argues that Islam can and should be reinterpreted constantly to meet the ever-changing needs of a dynamic society, even if these reinterpretations mean the occasional abandonment of certain deeply entrenched traditions.

## Religious minorities under the Islamic Republic

The conditions of Iran's various religious minority communities have varied both according to changing circumstances since the late 1970s and among themselves. The country is about ninety percent Shi'ite Muslim. Sunni Muslims account for perhaps another seven percent. Iran's Sunnis are mainly of non-Persian ethnicities, Iran today being only a little over fifty percent native Persian-speaking. Sunnis are mostly found among the Kurds of western Iran, the Baluch of the southeast, and the Turkmens in the northeast.

Sunni Muslims and Sufi orders have complained to international human rights organizations of discrimination by the officially Twelver Shi'ite state and harassment by ordinary citizens. Sunnis have not been allowed to build a mosque in the capital, and frequently perceive insults to Sunni Islam in the government-sponsored media. Government agents have been implicated in the assassinations of a number of Iranian Sunni religious leaders. Sufism has been generally discouraged, no doubt because of its occasional heterodox practices and the threat of charismatic leadership.

Among the non-Muslim groups, it could probably be said that Armenian Christians, having a four-hundred-year history of mostly manageable co-existence with Muslim Iranians, have fared the best. By contrast the Baha'is, as members of a religion not recognized by Islam, have suffered the most. All of Iran's non-Muslim religious communities have seen dwindling numbers, mainly through emigration to the US, Europe, and Australia.

The so-called Assembly of Experts which drafted the constitution of the Islamic Republic in 1979 included four non-Muslim delegates: one Zoroastrian, one Armenian, one Assyrian, and one Jew. Although in the end their inclusion was perhaps little more than a gesture of tokenism, Article 13 of the eventual constitution granted each of the recognized minority communities explicit recognition and protection. It reads: "Zoroastrian, Jewish and Christian Iranians are the only recognized religious minorities who are legally free in the practice of their religious ceremonies, on matters of personal status and education." Other non-Muslim Iranians, including Baha'is and Mandaeans, were implicitly denied these freedoms and protections. Although the Iranian parliament guarantees five seats for recognized religious minority communities – two for the Armenians, one for the Assyrians and Chaldeans, and one each for the Jews and Zoroastrians – in practice the guarantees provided in Article 13 of the constitution have been violated for all non-Muslim communities at one time or another.

A number of Islamic laws formally discriminate against non-Muslims. One that Iran's religious minorities find particularly egregious is the difference in "blood money" paid to the family of someone who has been unlawfully killed: the sum due to the family of a non-Muslim is half that accorded to the family of a Muslim. The non-Muslim parliamentarians have been actively lobbying for this law to be changed, however, and there are signs they may succeed.

Non-Muslims were the occasional target of attacks by fanatics in the early years of the revolution. Two Zoroastrian temples were desecrated in 1979, and in 1980 Armenian graveyards were vandalized in several cities. Revolutionary Guards broke into the Armenian cathedral in Tehran, and noticing a scantily clad Jesus in one of the paintings, called for the painter to return and add more clothing. In 1983 the government began appointing unsympathetic Muslim principals and teachers to serve in non-Muslim schools, and reduced the teaching of languages such as Armenian and Assyrian (Aramaic). Non-Muslims were discriminated against in the workplace, notably in the oil industry.

Since the revolution there has been an increased attention to "protecting" Muslims from the ritually unclean (from the Shi'ite point of view) contact of non-Muslims, even in the context of non-Muslim factory workers touching products that will be consumed by Muslims. Armenian-Iranian political scientist Eliz Sanasarian calls this heightened sensitivity "*nejasat* (impurity) consciousness."

In 1999, 2000, and 2001 the US Department of State designated Iran as a "country of particular concern" under the International Religious Freedom Act.[5] International refugee organizations have tended to be sympathetic to Iranian minorities claiming persecution, but it may be suspected that at least some of these claims are opportunistic. Although Iran's non-Muslims were undeniably subjected to great hardships, especially during the early years of the revolution, it should be acknowledged that Muslim Iranians also suffered from the excesses of revolutionary zealots and eight years of war with Iraq. While non-Muslims in Iran may have been occasionally singled out or denied certain rights and protections, the same is true for minority groups in virtually any society in times of severe social upheaval. Nevertheless, an overall assessment would suggest that in most respects Iran's non-Muslim communities are weaker today than they were prior to 1979.

## ZOROASTRIANS

Estimates of the current population of Zoroastrians vary widely. Worldwide the figures are claimed to be anywhere from 200,000 to three million. In Iran the number is said to be between 50,000 and 135,000. With the loosening of travel restrictions to Iran, Zoroastrians from around the world are making pilgrimages to the sacred shrine of Chak Chak some thirty miles north of Yazd, and several international Zoroastrian conferences in the 1990s drew attendees from a number of countries.

Although Zoroastrians faced most of the same kinds of bigotry and insecurity as other non-Muslim groups during the early 1980s, at the present time they enjoy a measure of official respect which can at times seem surprising. Zoroastrian celebrations are reported neutrally in the official press, and Zoroastrian leaders are now regularly invited to take part in government-sponsored conferences on religious themes.

I gave a public lecture in Esfahan in 2001 before a large audience in which there was one Zoroastrian. In the question and answer session after my talk, which was about environmental values in the world's religions, first a middle-aged woman in full Islamic garb rose to challenge me with the assertion that "Islam contains the perfect answer to all questions, including the environmental crisis." She wanted to go on but was quickly hushed by an irritated audience. Next the Zoroastrian stood up and made a similar claim about his own faith. He then proceeded to pontificate about his religion for at least forty minutes, while the audience listened quietly and patiently to all he had to say.

## JEWS

Iranians are a conspiracy-minded people, and Jews have long been seen as conspiracy's agents. Ruhollah Khomeini, during his years of exile in the 1960s and 1970s, often referred to the Pahlavi regime as being controlled by Zionists. Under the Islamic Republic the rhetoric on Jews has been highly mixed. On the one hand, religious leaders are generally quick to assert that Islam respects Judaism and that Jews are protected under Islamic law. At the same time, the impulse to see Jews behind every purported plot has continued. In principle Iran's religious leaders claim to distinguish between Iranian Jews who are honest and loyal to their country and those who secretly act on behalf of Israel, but in practice the distinction is not so clearly made.

In reality, of the three recognized religious minorities in the Islamic Republic, Jews have fared the worst. Nor has the government's animosity towards Jews been restricted to suspected Israeli spies within the country or support for radical Palestinian groups abroad. In March 2003 the government of Argentina released the details of an eight-year investigation into the 1994 bombing of a Buenos Aires Jewish center which killed eighty-five people. The investigation claimed that the attack, together with an earlier one in 1992 and a foiled attempt in 1996, were all orchestrated through the Iranian embassy in Buenos Aires and funded through a Swiss bank account controlled by Supreme Leader Ayatollah Ali Khamene'i.

Even under the comparatively progressive Khatami regime Jews in Iran have continued to suffer repression (though it is likely that these acts are carried out by Khatami's hardline opponents). In 1999 a group of thirteen Iranian Jews were arrested on charges of spying for Israel, once again bringing Iran the unwanted attention of international human rights groups. An estimated 20,000 to 30,000 Jews remain in Iran today, their numbers continuing to shrink through emigration.

CHRISTIANS

The Armenian population in Iran, which was over 300,000 before the revolution, now stands officially at 150,000 and may be even less. (Armenian leaders are reluctant to say, as they fear jeopardizing their two seats in parliament.) Even so, they remain the country's largest recognized non-Muslim community. The smaller Assyrian and Chaldean communities have dwindled even more sharply, and their combined number in Iran is probably less than 20,000. All three Christian groups have lost considerable numbers through emigration, mainly to California. They have also seen a decline in birthrates, in keeping with the overall national average. With the advent of an independent Armenian state following the collapse of the former Soviet Union in 1991 there has been an increase in travel and business networks between Armenians in Iran and Armenia.

While overall Armenians have suffered less discrimination than other non-Muslim groups since the revolution, they have had to struggle to maintain their rights to linguistic and religious education which the government has made occasional attempts to compromise. On the other hand, thanks to their historical cosmopolitanism and access to international networks, their special role in trade has been preserved. Many shops selling tourist items or international foods, for example, are Armenian-owned. Even so, the decline in numbers of foreign tourists since the revolution has hit Armenian merchants and craftspeople particularly hard. Recently some Armenians are said to have obtained government jobs, from which they were excluded after the 1979 revolution.

Because as Christians the Armenians are legally allowed to produce, sell, and consume alcoholic beverages among themselves (in principle because wine is required for holy communion), they have tended to control the illegal traffic in alcohol among Muslims as well. Once before a party in Tehran I was mystified by the hostess's frantic complaints that "the Armenian plumber" hadn't arrived yet. Not seeing a water leak anywhere, I failed to understand why she was so concerned. Then the "plumber" finally arrived; he opened his "plumber's kit," and began to stock the bar in time for the party.

The small numbers of Armenian Protestants – a legacy of European and American missionary efforts – have fared less well. Unlike the country's recognized Christian communities, Protestant and Catholic groups in Iran continue to proselytize (often conducting their services in Persian), and because they are under the jurisdiction of church administrations in Europe or the United States they are often accused of serving foreign interests. In 1994 the Armenian head of Iran's Council of Protestant Churches, Tateos Mikaelian, was murdered under mysterious circumstances.

Although Western missions of the nineteenth and twentieth centuries were technically allowed only to proselytize among non-Muslims, small numbers of Iranian Muslims did convert to Catholic and Protestant Christianity. Since Islam does not allow for apostasy, these conversions have not been recognized by the Islamic Republic. Thus, like the Baha'is, Christian converts have been denied the rights and protections theoretically afforded to recognized religious minorities. Furthermore, because of their foreign connections, Catholic and Protestant churches in Iran have been perceived as centers of espionage. Many have been closed down by the government.

In 1979 an Anglican minister (an Iranian) was murdered in Shiraz, and church properties were confiscated all over the country. Catholic missionary schools were likewise seized by the government. The case of Mehdi Dibaj, an Iranian convert to Protestantism who was arrested in 1983 and held for ten years before his trial for apostasy, gained international attention, but in 1994 he was assassinated nevertheless.

## BAHA'IS

Though it would be impossible to obtain reliable figures, Baha'is likely remain Iran's largest non-Muslim minority. An educated guess would put their numbers at somewhere around 300,000, but the true figure could well be much more or much less. Many Iranian Baha'is have emigrated to other countries (especially the United States), and many of those who remain dissimulate their true beliefs and outwardly pose as Muslims. Since 1983 Baha'is in Iran have been prohibited from assembling, forming administrative bodies, or maintaining contacts with Baha'is in other countries.

From the outset of the revolution Baha'is have been considered the paradigmatic infidels, suspected of turning Muslims from their faith and of acting as agents for foreign powers. As an unrecognized religious minority they have been without legal protection. They have been fired from their jobs and denied access to higher education. Baha'i assets, including land, holy sites, and cemeteries were seized by the government. Revolutionary Guards destroyed the house of the Bab in Shiraz in 1979. The following year all nine members of the Baha'i National Spiritual Assembly of Iran were arrested and presumably executed in secret. The following year eight of their nine successors were executed as well, accused of being spies. During the first five years of the revolution Amnesty International, the United Nations, and other organizations documented over two hundred executions of Baha'is in Iran.

As late as 1998 a Baha'i was executed on the charge of having converted a Muslim, and in 2000 a Baha'i cemetery in Abadeh was bulldozed. In 2002 the municipality of Tehran granted a small parcel of land to local Baha'is to use for burials; they are not allowed to perform Baha'i funerals there, however, or to put up individual grave markers. In cases where Baha'is are victims of murder or manslaughter, their relatives are not eligible for compensation. Baha'is are not allowed to attend public universities.

The position of the present Iranian government towards the Baha'i faith verges on the bizarre. Although their existence is acknowledged, Baha'is are not described as a religious group at all, but rather as an underground political movement bent on selling out the country's sovereignty. Official references to the Baha'i faith claim that it is an organization founded by the British in the nineteenth century as part of the latter's colonial project, aimed at the eventual takeover of Iran by foreign interests. In addition, because the shrine of Baha'u'llah and the Universal House of Justice happen to be located in what is now the state of Israel, Baha'is are readily accused of acting as agents of Zionism. Any admission of the Babi movement as arising from within messianic Shi'ism is entirely absent, and the explicit Baha'i tenet of political non-involvement is disregarded. The rabid hostility of the official view makes it essentially impossible within

Iran today to obtain anything approaching an accurate understanding of the Baha'i religion.

Nevertheless, under the Khatami regime the drastic strictures on Baha'is have been relieved somewhat, through indirect means. For example, the elimination in 2000 of the requirement to state one's religious affiliation on marriage forms allowed for the de facto registration of Baha'i marriages. Two Baha'is arrested in 1998 and originally condemned to death have both been released from prison.

MANDAEANS

The modern Mandaean community – the only ancient Gnostic group to survive up to the present day – is split between the province of Khuzestan in southwestern Iran (mainly the city of Ahvaz) and the marshes of southern Iraq. Iranian Mandaeans lost their status as a protected community after the 1979 revolution. This was theoretically restored by a *fatwa* (legal opinion) from Supreme Leader Ayatollah Ali Khamene'i in 1995, but has not yet been put into practice. Many, especially of the younger generation, have emigrated. There are significant Mandaean communities today in the United States – for example, in New York City, New Jersey, and San Diego – and in Australia. Mandaeans are prominent in the gold and silversmithing trades in both Iran and Iraq, and now in other countries as well. The actual number of Mandaeans is unknown, but may range from as low as 14,000 to as much as 100,000 or more worldwide.

Jorunn Buckley, a Norwegian-American scholar who has been working with Mandaeans for over thirty years, has been instrumental in bringing this tradition into the public awareness, even in Iran, where many scholars have told her they didn't know such a religion existed in their own country. Buckley has also brought Mandaeans to the attention of the international community, arguing for their recognition by international refugee organizations.

The future survival of this ancient religious community, which Buckley fears to be in jeopardy, is threatened by several factors. It is not possible to convert to Mandaism; one may only be born into it. Though Mandaeans have a long history of successfully keeping marriages within the tradition, endogamy has become increasingly difficult especially given the rate of emigration from their historical homelands.

There are other problems associated with emigration. Mandaean communities abroad lack both an adequate number of priests to perform their rituals, and consecrated places in which to perform them. Copies of Mandaean sacred texts are limited, and knowledge of the language is on the wane. Recently there have been attempts to remedy these problems, through the relocation of priests, the copying of texts, and the seeking out of appropriate locations for baptisms. The possibility of allowing conversions through marriage has been advocated by laypeople but is staunchly rejected by Mandaean priests.

## Conclusion

Iran's Islamic revolution has brought about many paradoxes. Twelver Shi'ite political theory has been dramatically revised, and an historically underdog religious ethos has found itself in a position of temporal authority and accountability. After more than two decades the often hysterical and paranoid voices of religious extremism and intolerance have somewhat subsided (though they have not disappeared), especially since the election of Mohammad Khatami as president in 1997. The fear that members of religious minorities are acting as spies for foreign governments persists, though one wonders what sort of valuable intelligence people who have been so utterly marginalized could possibly provide. When was the last time a Jew or Baha'i in Iran was granted security clearance to a government agency or sensitive site?

At the same time the interest of many Iranians in religions other than Shi'i Islam has seen an increase, due at least in part to an ever-growing obsession with an outside world relatively few Iranians can visit and experience for themselves. Part of this may be a reaction against the religious ideology of a regime that has been losing popularity and is blamed for the continued sense of isolation and deprivation that many Iranians feel. At a social event in early 2003 a famous Iranian actress, who spends much time in the United States but continues to work in Iran, somewhat defiantly informed me that she is a practicing Buddhist.

But it is also true that curiosity about other religions does not necessarily imply a rejection of Islam. After I gave a lecture at Tehran University in 2001, a young woman approached me and asked if I had ever heard of Transcendental Meditation. She informed me that TM centers have proliferated in Tehran, but that young Iranians today see no contradiction in practicing this technique while remaining devout Muslims.

Even among the younger generation of seminary students one can see a marked fascination with the study of other religions. This includes the study of Buddhism, which Muslims have long considered the archetypical "idol-worshipping" religion. (The Baha'i faith remains a taboo subject, however.) A new Center for the Study of Religions and Sects located in the very heart of Qom has attracted a number of bright young seminarians from the nearby *hawzeh*. It possesses an impressive and up-to-date collection of library resources, including the latest Western scholarship from university presses. The Center publishes a scholarly journal devoted to the comparative study of religions, *Haft Asman* (Seven Heavens), and has helped organize a number of international conferences.

Such trends would seem to indicate that the intellectual climate in Iran today is becoming more open to learning about religions other than the official one. While an explicitly Islamic state cannot allow Muslims to convert to other religions, it may be hoped that in the coming years Iranians will have more opportunities to pursue their curiosity about the world's various faiths in a spirit of objectivity and respect, and to contemplate in the broadest way the immense role their own culture has played in the history of world religions.

# Glossary

*ahura*

Beneficent deity; Ahura Mazda/Ormazd (Lord Wisdom) being the central god of Zoroastrianism

**Airyana Vaejah**

Name given by proto-Iranians to their ancestral homeland

**Angra Mainyu/Ahriman**

Evil deity in Zoroastrianism

**Aryan** (*\*airyo*)

Self-designation of prehistoric Indo-European speakers

*asha* (*arta*)

The principle of truth, uprightness, and cosmic order

**Avesta**

Sacred book of Zoroastrianism, compiled during the third century CE from much older oral material

*daeva*

Demon, evil deity (cf. modern Persian *div*, English "devil")

*dharma*

In Buddhism, refers to the teaching of the Buddha

*dhimmi* (*zemmi*)

Member of a non-Muslim religious community recognized and accorded protection under Islam

*din*

(Pronounced "deen"); the personal, inner dimension of religion

*drug*

(Pronounced "droog"); the opposite of *asha*, often translated as "The Lie" (cf. modern Persian *dorugh*, "lie")

**Gathas**

The seventeen oldest hymns of the Avesta, believed to have been composed by Zoroaster himself

*hadith*

A report about the words or deeds of Muhammad; supplementing the Qur'an, the major source for Islamic law

*haoma* (*soma*)

Sacred hallucinogenic beverage of the ancient Indo-Iranians, used in ritual sacrifice

**Imam**

For Shi'ite Muslims, the divinely guided rightful spiritual and temporal leader of Muslims; for Sunnis, an honorific term applicable to any religious leader

**Indo-European**

Family of languages, distributed in historical times from Europe to India (including both English and Persian), descended from a common ancestor language referred to as Proto-Indo-European

**Isma'ili**

A Shi'ite Muslim who follows the line of imams descended from the sixth Imam Ja'far's son Isma'il; also known as "Seveners" or, often pejoratively, as "Esotericists" (*batiniyya*)

*jizya*

Poll-tax levied by Muslim governments on members of recognized non-Muslim communities *khvarna (farr)*

Divine blessing, symbolized by a halo of fire

*mahdi*

Islamic eschatological savior figure

*mainyu*

Spirit beings, believed by ancient Iranians to inhere in natural phenomena and also in abstract qualities

*mobad*

Magus, Zoroastrian priest

**Noruz**

Literally "new day," the major Iranian festival, celebrated at the spring equinox; the first day of the year in the Persian calendar

**Parsee**

Term by which Zoroastrians are known in India

**Sakas (Scythians)**

Nomadic, often warlike Iranian tribes of ancient Central Eurasia

**Saoshyant**

Zoroastrian savior figure, probable inspiration of Jewish notion of messiah

*shari'a*

Islamic legal code, covering all aspects of human behavior

**Shi'ite**

A Muslim who accepts the spiritual (and, in theory, the temporal) authority of the line of descendants of Muhammad known as the Imams, and follows the Ja'fari school of law

*sramana*

Buddhist monk

*stupa*

Buddhist shrine, often believed to house relic of the Buddha

**Sufi**

Muslim mystic, generally a follower of a charismatic teacher (called a *pir* or *shaykh*)

**Sunni**

A Muslim who follows one of the four schools of law accepted by the majority of Muslims: the Shafi'i, the Maliki, the Hanafi, or the Hanbali

**Twelver (*Ithna 'Ashari*)**

A Shi'ite Muslim who follows the line of imams descended from the sixth Imam Ja'far's son Musa al-Kazim; *Ithna 'Ashari* Shi'ism is the larger of the two main Shi'ite sects and the official religion of the Islamic Republic of Iran

**'*ulema*' (sing. *'alim*)**

Islamic legal scholars

*vihara*

Buddhist monastery

*zindiq*

Heretic, Manichaean

**Zurvan**

God of time and fate; believed by many in Sasanian times to be the primordial deity from whom both Ahura Mazda and Angra Mainyu emerged

# Notes

CHAPTER 1: THE ORIGINS OF IRANIAN RELIGION

1. Other contemporary Iranian languages include Kurdish, Baluch, Pashtu, Ossetian, Pamiri, and many others.
2. "Indo-European" refers to a group of languages, including most of the languages of Europe plus many of Iran, South Asia, and elsewhere, which can be shown to have derived from a common ancestor language referred to by scholars as "Proto-Indo-European."
3. An asterisk signals a reconstructed word not attested in any written sources.
4. In terms of developmental anthropology, pastoralism is said to follow agriculture, and not to precede it. Presumably the ancestors of the PIEs practiced agriculture, but seeing the ecological constraints of their steppe environment, the PIEs largely abandoned agriculture in favor of a pastoral nomadic economy augmented by raiding.
5. The tripartite nature of PIE society has been most fully theorized by the French comparative mythologist Georges Dumézil and his students. Others have challenged this approach, however, arguing that the paradigm is not unique to Indo-Europeans.
6. In deference to the fact that non-Christians have now widely adopted the "Christian" calendar, the terms BCE ("Before the Common Era") and CE ("Common Era") are used in place of BC ("Before Christ") and AD ("Anno Domini," "Year of Our Lord").
7. Though the Rig Veda and other later Vedas are often among the sacred scriptures memorized by Hindu Brahmin priests, their role in

Hinduism is fairly circumscribed and in no way analogous to the central and normative role of the Bible or the Qur'an in Judaism, Christianity, and Islam, or even the Avesta in Zoroastrianism. The attempts of Hindu nationalists in India today to endow the Vedas with such a status is very recent, and certainly owes something to Western notions of what constitutes religion.

8. *The Rig Veda*, translated by Wendy Doniger O'Flaherty (New York: Penguin Books, 1981), hymn no. 10.119, pp. 131–132.
9. It is probably significant that the term "shaman" is a word originating from the Eurasian steppes, albeit a much later appearance in Altaic – that is, non-Indo-European – language.
10. Or possibly down the western side of the Caspian and over the Caucasus, or even by both routes.
11. *Karshvar*; the modern Persian word, *keshvar*, means "country."
12. The earliest written references to Indo-Iranians are cuneiform texts from Mesopotamia. One document, a treaty dating to about 1370 BCE, mentions Mitra, Varuna, and Indra.
13. *Aitareya Brahmana*, translated by Martin Haug (New York: AMS Press, 1974), 2.6.

CHAPTER 2: ZOROASTRIANISM

1. Adapted from the translation in William W. Malandra, *An Introduction to Ancient Iranian Religion* (Minneapolis: University of Minnesota Press, 1983), pp. 38–39.
2. Mas'udi, *Muruj al-dhahab*, v. 1, p. 289; quoted in Michael G. Morony, *Iraq After the Muslim Conquest* (Princeton, NJ: Princeton University Press, 1984), p. 30.
3. A. S. Melikian-Chirvani, "The Wine Birds of Iran from Pre-Achaemenid to Islamic Times," *Bulletin of the Asia Institute*, 9, 1995, p. 41.
4. *Denkard*, edited with English translation by P. B. and D. P. Sanjana, 19 vols. (Bombay, 1928), 413:2–8.

CHAPTER 3: JUDAISM

1. Hooshang Ebrami, "Introduction," in Habib Levy, *Comprehensive History of the Jews of Iran: The Outset of the Diaspora* (Costa Mesa, CA: Mazda Publishers, 1999), p. xvi.
2. Esther 9:24–28, *The Tanakh* (Philadelphia: Jewish Publication Society, 1985).

3. Ebrami, p. xv.
4. Jacob Neusner, *History of the Jews in Babylonia* (Leiden: Brill, 1970), vol. 5, pp. 11–14.
5. Levy, *Comprehensive History of the Jews of Iran*, p. 255.
6. Babai b. Lutf, *Kitab-e Anusi*, translated by Vera Basch Moreen in *In Queen Esther's Garden: An Anthology of Judeo-Persian Literature* (New Haven, CT: Yale University Press, 2000), p. 281.

CHAPTER 4: BUDDHISM

1. The term "buddha" means "enlightened one."
2. Mariko Namba Walter, "Buddhism in Western Central Asia," paper presented at the 111th American Historical Association annual conference, Seattle 1998.
3. "Statues in Iran Challenge Theories on Buddhism's Spread," *The Japan Times*, 14 May 2002.
4. The existence of a Persian meaning for this term, "new spring," is most likely coincidental.
5. Samuel Beal, *Buddhist Records of the Western World* (New Delhi: Oriental Reprints, 1969 [1888]), pp. 44–45.
6. Ibid., pp. 45–46.
7. Mas'udi, *Muruj al-dhahab*, edited and translated by Barbier de Meynard (Paris, 1965), vol. 4, p. 79; cited in A. S. Melikian-Chirvani, "L'évocation littéraire du bouddhisme dans l'Iran musulman," *Le monde iranien et l'Islam*, 2, 1974, p. 20.
8. Melikian-Chirvani, "L'évocation littéraire du bouddhisme," p. 37.
9. Ibid., 57.
10. Iwamoto Yutaka, *Jigoku meguri no bungaku* (Tokyo: Kaimei shoten, 1979), pp. 184–199; cited in Stephen F. Teiser, *The Ghost Festival in Medieval China* (Princeton, NJ: Princeton University Press, 1988), p. 24.

CHAPTER 5: CHRISTIANITY

1. Hans-Joachim Klimkeit, "Christians in Persia," in Ian Gillman and Hans-Joachim Klimkeit, *Christians in Asia Before 1500* (Ann Arbor, University of Michigan Press, 1999).
2. Ian Gillman and Hans-Joachim Klimkeit, *Christians in Asia Before 1500*, p. 112.
3. The official adoption of Christianity in Armenia has traditionally been dated at 301 CE, but recently scholars have come to posit a date of 314–315 as more likely.

4. Tabari's *History*, cited in Mary Boyce, *Zoroastrians: Their Religious Beliefs and Practices* (London: Routledge and Kegan Paul, 1979), p. 141.

5. James R. Russell, "Christianity in Pre-Islamic Persia: Literary Sources," *Encyclopedia Iranica*, v. 5, p. 526.

6. Taken from Aphrahat, "On the Paschal Sacrifice," in *Demonstrations*, translated by Jacob Neusner in *Aphrahat and Judaism: the Christian-Jewish Argument in Fourth-Century Iran* (Leiden: Brill, 1971), pp. 34, 36, 40.

7. *Synodicon Orientale ou Recueil de Synodes Nestoriens*, edited and translated by Jean-Baptiste Chabot (Paris: Imprimérie nationale, 1902), Canon 25, pp. 417–418.

8. *Synodicon Orientale*, Canon 14, p. 488.

9. *Ausgewählte Akten persischer Märtyrer*, translated by O. Braun (Bibliothek der Kirchenväter, 1915), v. 22, p. 109; cited in Boyce, *Zoroastrians*, p. 140.

10. Cited in Gillman and Klimkeit, *Christians in Asia Before 1500*, p. 130.

11. In an interesting precedent, the Sasanian emperor Shapur II transferred much of the Christian and Jewish population of Armenia to Esfahan in 365 CE, in an apparent attempt to weaken Armenia's economy and make it more dependent on Iran.

CHAPTER 6: GNOSTIC TRADITIONS

1. See Şinasi Gündüz, *The Knowledge of Life: The Origins and Early History of the Mandaeans and Their Relationship to the Sabeans of the Qur'an and the Harranians* (Oxford: Oxford University Press, 1994).

2. Cited in Jason David BeDuhn, *The Manichaean Body: In Discipline and Ritual* (Baltimore: Johns Hopkins University Press, 2000), p. 6.

3. Qadi Ahmad of Qom, *Calligraphers and Painters: A Treatise by Qadi Ahmad, son of Mir Munshi (circa A.H. 1015/A.D. 1606)*, trans. Vladimir Minorsky (Washington, DC: Smithsonian Institution, 1959), pp. 159, 174, 177–180, 192.

4. From Hans-Joachim Klimkeit, *Gnosis on the Silk Road* (San Francisco: Harper, 1996), p. 38.

5. Augustine of Hippo, *Contra Faustum*, in Philip Schaff, ed., *Nicene and Post-Nicene Fathers* (Grand Rapids, MI: Eerdmans, 1983), v. 4, 5.10.

6. Samuel N. C. Lieu, *Manichaeism in Mesopotamia and the Roman East* (Leiden: Brill, 1999), p. 31.
7. Sarah Stroumsa and Gedaliahu G. Stroumsa, "Aspects of Anti-Manichaean Polemics in Late Antiquity and Under Early Islam," *Harvard Theological Review*, 81/1, 1988, p. 53.
8. *The Epic of the Kings*, translated by Reuben Levy (London: Routledge and Kegan Paul, 1967), p. 319.
9. Joseph Wolff, *Narrative of a Mission to Bokhara* (London, 1848), pp. 297–298.

CHAPTER 7: ISLAM

1. A revisionist view which sought to diminish the Iranian character of the Abbasid revolution and subsequent empire, espoused by such scholars as D. C. Dennett, Abd al-Aziz Duri, Faruq Omar, Moshe Sharon, Jacob Lassner, and M. A. Shaban, has been discredited by Ehsan Yarshater and others on the basis of strong primary source evidence.
2. Wheeler M. Thackston, "The Poetry of Shah Esma'il I," *Asian Art*, Fall 1988, p. 57.
3. Ibid., pp. 56–57.
4. Quoted in Donald Wilber, *Persian Gardens and Garden Pavilions*, second edition (Washington, DC: Dumbarton Oaks, 1979), pp. 19–20.

CHAPTER 8: THE BABI MOVEMENT AND THE BAHA'I FAITH

1. E. G. Browne, *A Traveller's Narrative Written to Illustrate the Episode of the Bab* (Amsterdam: Philo Press, 1975 [1886]), v. 2, p. xl.
2. Baha'u'llah, in *The Compilation of Compilations*, 2:358.
3. Baha'u'llah, in Ahmad Yazdani, *Maqam va huquq-e zan dar diyanat-e baha'i* (Tehran: Lajneh-e melli-ye nashr-e athar-e amri, 107/1951), p. 12.
4. Baha'u'llah, *Majmu'eh'i az alvah-e mobarakeh* (Tehran: Mo'assaseh-e melli-ye matbu'at-e amri, 132/1976), p. 115.

CHAPTER 9: RELIGIONS IN IRAN TODAY

1. Twelver Shi'is traditionally followed the rulings of the highest-ranking legal scholar, known as the *marja'-e taqlid* ("model for

imitation"), but following the death of the *marja'* Ayatollah Borujerdi in 1961 Twelver Shi'ites gave their allegiance to several different leading clerics, of which Khomeini was one.

2.  Khatami's position, that of a believer in the system but who does not support its imposition by force, echoes that of Mikhail Gorbachev, the last premier of the Soviet Union. It is sad to think that, like Gorbachev, Khatami's contribution to the liberation of his own society may be quickly forgotten once it is achieved.

3.  Private conversations with the author, summer 2001.

4.  One could say even further that the US's ongoing unquestioned support for Israel despite the acknowledged excesses of the latter is not materially different from Iran's of the not untarnished Palestinian cause; the US and Iran just happen to be on different sides of the issue. It may also be noted that outside the United States, throughout the world many people see the US and Israel as the leading state-sponsors of terrorism, by the very same criteria the US applies to the "axis of evil" and other countries such as Syria or Libya. Even within the United States, polls show a majority of Americans consider the US to be the single greatest threat to world peace. Americanist ideologues thus face an ongoing credibility problem in winning global support for their international policing policies.

5.  *International Religious Freedom Report: Iran* (Washington, DC: Department of State, 7 October 2002).

# Bibliographic Essay

GENERAL WORKS

Alessandro Bausani's 1959 survey *Persia Religiosa*, translated into English as *Religion in Iran: From Zoroaster to Baha'ullah* (New York: Bibliotheca Persica, 2000), remains the most extensive scholarly discussion of the history of Iranian religions, though it neglects Judaism, Christianity, and Buddhism. My own previous book, *Religions of the Silk Road: Overland Trade and Cultural Exchange from Antiquity to the Fifteenth Century* (New York: St. Martin's Press, 1999), highlights the role of Iranian peoples in the transmission of world religions via the overland trade routes of Asia throughout premodern history.

Ehsan Yarshater, who has been one of the major figures in developing the field of Iranian Studies in the United States, has written on all aspects of Iranian history and culture, especially the Persian language and literary tradition. Yarshater edited *The Cambridge History of Iran*, v. 3, *The Seleucid, Parthian, and Sasanian Periods* (Cambridge: Cambridge University Press, 1983), which includes a large section on religions. The monumental *Encyclopedia Iranica* (London: Routledge and Kegan Paul, 1982–1989 and New York: Bibliotheca Persica, 1992–present; 11 vols. to date), also edited by Yarshater and still in progress, contains a number of entries on Iran's various religious traditions. Many entries are accessible online through the encyclopedia's website at <www.iranica.com>. The

*Encyclopedia of Religion*, edited by Mircea Eliade, 16 vols. (New York: Macmillan, 1987) also has many entries related to Iran, as does the now dated *Encyclopedia of Religion and Ethics*, edited by James Hastings (New York: Scribners, 1928). Finally, there are sections on religions in the five-volume *History of Civilizations of Central Asia* (Paris: Unesco, 1992–). The *Bulletin of the Asia Institute* regularly features scholarly articles of relevance to religions of Iran especially in the ancient period.

Richard N. Frye remains the most eminent living American scholar of Iran. Among his many books are *The Heritage of Persia* (London: Weidenfeld & Nicolson, 1963) and *The Golden Age of Persia* (London: Weidenfeld & Nicolson, 1975). He also edited *The Cambridge History of Iran*, v. 4, *From the Arab Invasion to the Seljuks* (Cambridge: Cambridge University Press, 1975). A more recent general history of Iran, weighted toward the modern period, is Elton Daniel, *The History of Iran* (Westport, CT: Greenwood Press, 2001).

Some of the major Classical Muslim sources which include mention of religions other than Islam have appeared in English translations. Among the most important are Ibn Nadim [Abu'l-Faraj Muhammad ibn Ishaq al-Warraq], *Fihrist al-'ulum*, translated by B. Dodge, *The Fihrist of al-Nadim: A Tenth Century Survey of Muslim Culture*, 2 vols. (New York: Columbia University Press, 1970) and Abu Rayhan Biruni, *Athar-al-baqiya*, translated by C. Edward Sachau as *The Chronology of Ancient Nations* (reprint edition, Lahore: Hijra International Publishers, 1983 [1879]).

CHAPTER 1: THE ORIGINS OF IRANIAN RELIGION

The standard work on Indo-European origins is J. P. Mallory, *In Search of the Indo-Europeans: Language, Archaeology, and Myth* (London: Thames & Hudson, 1989). The approach of Georges Dumézil is summarized in his *Mythe et Epopée*, 3 vols. (Paris: Gallimard, 1968–1973), portions of which have appeared in English translations. Bruce Lincoln is perhaps the leading contemporary scholar on Indo-European religion. Among his many works the most relevant to this discussion are *Myth, Cosmos, and Society: Indo-European Themes of Creation and Destruction* (Cambridge, MA: Harvard University Press, 1986) and *Priests, Warriors, and Cattle: A Study in the*

*Ecology of Religions* (Berkeley: University of California Press, 1981).

There is still debate over the "original" homeland of the PIEs. The greatest weight of evidence has been provided by Lithuanian archeologist Marija Gimbutas. See for example her *The Gods and Goddesses of Old Europe* (Berkeley, CA: University of California Press, 1974) and *Bronze Age Cultures of Central and Eastern Europe* (The Hague: Mouton, 1965). A concise source on Indo-European words is *The American Heritage Dictionary of Indo-European Roots*, edited by Calvert Watkins, 2nd ed. (Boston: Houghton Mifflin, 2000). An extensive study on the substance known as *haoma* (*soma*) is David S. Flattery and Martin Schwartz, *Haoma and Harmaline: The Botanical Identity of the Indo-Iranian Sacred Hallucinogen "Soma" and Its Legacy in Religion, Language, and Middle Eastern Folklore* (Berkeley: University of California Press, 1989).

CHAPTER 2: ZOROASTRIANISM

One of the most prolific contemporary scholars of Zoroastrianism is Mary Boyce. Her *A History of Zoroastrianism*, 3 vols. to date (Leiden: Brill, 1975–1991), is the most thorough exposition of the subject, summarized and revised somewhat in her more concise treatment, *Zoroastrianism: Its Antiquity and Constant Vigour* (Costa Mesa: Mazda Publishers, 1992). Boyce's scholarship is colored, however, by her intense identification with her subject. Her dating of Zoroaster's lifetime is criticized by Gherardo Gnoli in *Zoroaster in History* (New York: Bibliotheca Persica, 2000). Jean Kellens' work, which is mainly in French, includes *Qui était Zarathustra?* (Liège: Faculté de Philosophie et Lettres, 1993).

Perhaps the best-known ancient Greek source on Iran is Herodotus, *The Histories*, translated by Aubrey de Sélincourt, revised by A. R. Burn (New York: Penguin, 1972). A discussion of Roman Mithraism's Iranian origins can be found in A. D. H. Bivar, *The Personalities of Mithra in Archaeology and Literature* (New York: Bibliotheca Persica, 1998); see also the entry by R. Beck at <www.iranica.com>.

Jamsheed Choksy's *Conflict and Cooperation* (New York: Columbia University Press, 1997) explores the dynamics between Zoroastrians and Muslims during the first centuries of Islam in Iran, based mainly on Zoroastrian sources. Books describing modern Zoroastrian communities in Iran include assassinated parliamentarian Keikhosrow Shahrokh's *The Memoirs of Keikhosrow Shahrokh*, edited by Shahrokh Shahrokh and Rashna Writer (Lewiston, NY: Edwin Mellen Press, 1995) and Rashna Writer, *Contemporary Zoroastrians: An Unstructured Nation* (Lanham, MD: University Press of America, 1993). Keikhosrow Shahrokh's half-English granddaughter has also published an interesting memoir, *The Dance of the Rose and the Nightingale* (Syracuse, NY: Syracuse University Press, 2002). Sven Hartman's study, *Parsism, the Religion of Zoroaster* (Leiden: Brill, 1980), focuses on Indian communities.

CHAPTER 3: JUDAISM

Though not a work of objective scholarship, the most complete survey of Jewish history in Iran is Habib Levy's 1960 opus in three volumes, *Tarikh-e Yahud-e Iran*, an abridged English translation of which has been published as the *Comprehensive History of the Jews of Iran: The Outset of the Diaspora* (Costa Mesa, CA: Mazda Publishers, 1999). Many specialized articles on various aspects of Iran's connection with Judaism have been collected in Shaul Shaked and Amnon Metzer, eds., *Irano-Judaica*, 3 vols. to date (Jerusalem: Ben-Zvi Institute, 1982–1994) and in Amnon Metzer, ed., *Padyavand*, 2 vols. to date (Costa Mesa: Mazda Publishers, 1994–1998). Another collection of essays is Houman Sarshar, ed., *Esther's Children: The Jews of Iran: Their Story, Their History, Their Lives* (Philadelphia: Jewish Publication Society, 2002).

Jacob Neusner's five-volume *History of the Jews in Babylonia* (Leiden: Brill, 1965–1970) is a comprehensive scholarly study of all aspects of Jewish life and culture during Parthian and Sasanian times. A one-volume redaction appeared as *Judaism, Christianity, and Zoroastrianism in Talmudic Babylonia* (Lanham, MD: University Press of America, 1986). A related study, *Aphrahat and Judaism: the Christian-Jewish Argument in Fourth-Century Iran* (Leiden: Brill, 1971) gives a translation of and commentary on a major Christian polemic against Judaism.

The Iranian-Jewish experience is the subject of much of Iranian-American novelist Gina B. Nahai's work. Her *Cry of the Peacock* (New York: Washington Square, 1991) is set against the past several centuries of Jewish history in Iran. A good survey of Iranian-Jewish literature in English translation is Vera Basch Moreen, trans., *In Queen Esther's Garden: An Anthology of Judeo-Persian Literature* (New Haven, CT: Yale University Press, 2000).

CHAPTER 4: BUDDHISM

The scholarship on Iranian Buddhism is extremely thin. Apart from C. S. Upasak's geographically constrained *Buddhism in Afghanistan* (Varanasi: Central Institute of Higher Tibetan Studies, 1990), to date there are no book-length treatments of Buddhism in the Iranian world. Ronald Emmerick, who is the major contemporary scholar of Buddhism among Iranian peoples, has contributed articles to several encyclopedias, though his work, mainly philological, focuses primarily on Iranian-speakers east of Iran such as the Khotanese Sakas. The best overall survey of Iranian influences in Buddhism is David Alan Scott, "The Iranian Face of Buddhism," *East and West*, 40, 1990, pp. 43–77.

*The World of Buddhism*, edited by Heinz Bechert and Richard Gombrich (London: Thames & Hudson, 1984), contains an important chapter by Oskar von Hinüber on "Expansion to the North: Afghanistan and Central Asia" (pp. 99–107). The *Encyclopaedia of Buddhism*, edited by G. P. Malalasekera (Columbo, 1979), likewise contains an entry on "Central Asia" by B. A. Litvinsky (v. 4, fasc. 1, pp. 21–52). The *Encyclopaedia Iranica* has several entries related to Buddhism in Iran. The Chinese travel accounts of Faxian, Songyun and Xuanzang, which give details on the extent of Buddhism in eastern Iran during the Sasanian period, are available in the English translation of Samuel Beal, *Buddhist Records of the Western World* (New Delhi: Oriental Reprints, 1969 [1888]). Xuanzang's experiences are retold in the very readable account of Sally Hovey Wriggins, *Xuanzang: A Buddhist Pilgrim on the Silk Road* (Boulder, CO: Westview Press, 1996).

Among the specialized studies appearing in scholarly journals are Sasaki Shizuka, "A Study on the Origin of Mahayana Buddhism," *The Eastern Buddhist*, 30/1, 1997, pp. 79–113; G. Koshelenko, "The Beginnings of Buddhism in Margiana," *Acta Antiqua Academiae Scientarum Hungaricae*, 14, 1966, pp. 175–183; A. S. Melikian-Chirvani, "L'évocation littéraire du bouddhisme dans l'Iran musulman," *Le monde iranien et l'Islam*, 2, 1974, pp. 1–72 and idem., "Recherches sur l'architecture de l'Iran bouddhique I: Essai sur les origins et le symbolisme du stupa iranien," *Le monde iranien et l'Islam*, 4, 1975, pp. 1–61; Warwick Ball, "Two Aspects of Iranian Buddhism," *Bulletin of the Asia Institute*, 4, 1976, pp. 103–163 and idem., "Some Rock-cut Monuments in Southern Iran," *Iran*, 24, 1986, pp. 95–115; B. Ya. Stavisky, "Kara Tepe in Old Termez: A Buddhist Religious Centre of the Kushan Period on the Bank of the Oxus," in J. Harmatta, ed., *From Hecataeus to Al-Huwarizmi: Bactrian, Pahlavi, Sogdian, Persian, Sanskrit, Syriac, Arabic, Chinese, Greek and Latin Sources for the History of Pre-Islamic Central Asia* (Budapest: Academiai Kiado, 1984), pp. 95–135; and Richard W. Bulliet, "Naw Bahar and the Survival of Iranian Buddhism," *Iran*, 14, 1976, pp. 140–145. Important research by David A. Utz and by Mariko Namba Walter, both of whom have worked on the early Buddhist tradition in Iranian Central Asia, unfortunately remains mostly unpublished.

CHAPTER 5: CHRISTIANITY

Most research on Iranian Christianity is both outdated and polemical, coming out of the nineteenth-century European missionary tradition which saw Iranian Christians as something of a lost tribe, to be both rescued from obscurity and corrected in their own deviant beliefs. The last scholarly effort of the late Hans-Joachim Klimkeit, a chapter on "Christians in Persia" in Ian Gillman and Hans-Joachim Klimkeit, *Christians in Asia Before 1500* (Ann Arbor: University of Michigan Press, 1999), offers the most reliable short survey of the subject for the pre-modern period. The chapter on Christianity in Arthur Christensen's *L'Iran sous les Sassanides* (Copenhagen: Munksgaard, 1944) is still useful, though a number of Christensen's conclusions have been challenged by more recent scholars.

Like Klimkeit, the Danish scholar Jes P. Asmussen, most of whose writings are in English, has written on both Manichaeism and Iranian Christianity. The *Encyclopedia Iranica* contains several entries on Christianity, notably those of James Russell, a specialist on Armenia, and Nicholas Sims-Williams, whose major focus is Sogdian. A. V. Williams, "Zoroastrians and Christians in Sasanian Iran," *Bulletin of the John Rylands Library*, 78/3, 1996, pp. 37–53, gives a good overview of intercommunal polemics with many citations from Christian texts.

An important primary source on eastern Christianity from the early Islamic period is *The Chronography of Gregory Abu'l Faraj*, translated by E. A. T. Wallis Budge, 2 vols. (London: Oxford University Press, 1932). Muslim sources such as the *Fihrist* of Ibn Nadim and the *Athar-al-baqiya* of Abu Rayhan Biruni also mention Christian communities in the early Muslim world. For the modern period, John Joseph has updated his 1961 survey of Assyrian Christians in a revised edition, *The Modern Assyrians of the Middle East: Encounters with Western Christian Missions, Archaeologists, and Colonial Powers* (Leiden: Brill, 2000).

CHAPTER 6: GNOSTIC TRADITIONS

The standard works on Gnosis in its various forms are Kurt Rudolph, *Gnosis: The Nature and History of Gnosticism* (San Francisco: Harper & Row, 1983) and Hans Jonas, *The Gnostic Religion: The Message of the Alien God and the Beginnings of Christianity*, 2nd ed. (London: Routledge, 1992 [1963]). H.-J. Klimkeit's *Gnosis on the Silk Road* (San Francisco: Harper, 1993) contains an extensive and varied collection of Manichaean texts translated into English. Another contemporary scholar of Manichaeism is Samuel N. C. Lieu, whose books include *Manichaeism in Central Asia and China* (Leiden: Brill, 1998), *Manichaeism in Mesopotamia and the Roman East* (Leiden: Brill, 1994), and *Manichaeism in the Later Roman Empire and Medieval China* (Tübingen: Mohr, 1992 [1985]).

Jason David BeDuhn reconstructs the life of Manichaean communities in *The Manichaean Body: In Discipline and Ritual* (Baltimore: Johns Hopkins University Press, 2000). Paul Mirecki and Jason BeDuhn have also edited two volumes of specialized studies on various aspects of Manichaeism: *Emerging From Darkness: Studies in the Recovery of Manichaean Sources* (Leiden: Brill, 1997) and *The Light and the Darkness: Studies in Manichaeism and its World* (Leiden: Brill, 2001). Lebanese novelist Amin Maalouf's *Gardens of Light* (New York: Interlink Books, 1999) is an entertaining and well-researched fictional portrayal of the life of Mani.

The most important contemporary scholar of Mandaeism is Jorunn Jacobsen Buckley. Her recent book, *The Mandaeans* (New

York: Oxford University Press, 2002), which summarizes thirty years of study, is a fascinating work of ethnography. Italian scholar Edmondo Lupieri's work has recently been published in English translation as *The Mandaeans: The Last Gnostics* (Grand Rapids, MI: Eerdmans, 2002). E. S. Drower's classic study, *The Mandaeans of Iraq and Iran: Their Cults, Customs, Magic, Legends, and Folklore*, originally published in 1937, is still an important resource and has recently been reprinted (Gorgias Press, 2002). M. Firouzandeh and A. Tahvildar's *Baptists in Iran* (Tehran: Key Press, 2001) is a trilingual book of photographs of Mandaeans.

Mazdakism has been discussed most notably by A. Christiansen *La Régne du roi Kawadh I et le communisme mazdakite* (Copenhagen, 1925), G.-H. Sadighi, *Les Mouvements réligieux iraniens au Iie et IIIe siècle de l'hégire* (Paris: Les Presses Modernes, 1938), O. Klima, *Mazdak: Geschichte einer sozialen Bewegung im sassanidischen Persien* (Prague, 1957), Ehsan Yarshater in *Encyclopedia of Iran*, v. 3, pp. 991–1024, and Wilferd Madelung, "Mazdakism and the Khurramiyya," in *Religious Trends in Early Islamic Iran* (Albany, NY: SUNY Press, 1988), pp. 1–12.

CHAPTER 7: ISLAM

The role of Iranians in shaping Muslim civilization is the focus of *The Persian Presence in the Islamic World* (Cambridge: Cambridge University Press, 1998), edited by Richard G. Hovannisian and Georges Sabagh. Ehsan Yarshater's title essay fills half the book, and is supplemented by shorter specialized chapters.

Marshall Hodgson, *The Venture of Islam*, 3 vols. (Chicago: University of Chicago Press, 1974) is the best scholarly survey of the rise of Islamic civilization. Hodgson devotes considerable attention to the Iranian world and its contribution to the development of Islamic civilization. Other useful surveys are Ira M. Lapidus, *A History of Islamic Societies*, 2nd ed. (Cambridge: Cambridge University Press, 2002 [1988]) and R. Stephen Humphreys, *Islamic History: A Framework for Inquiry* (Princeton: Princeton University Press, 1991). Richard N. Frye's *The Golden Age of Persia* and *Bukhara, the Medieval Achievement* both deal specifically with this issue. Sectarian movements are discussed in Wilferd Madelung, *Religious Trends in Early Islamic Iran* (Albany, NY: SUNY Press, 1988).

Richard W. Bulliet has shed much light on the conversion of Iranians to Islam during the seventh to tenth centuries in his books *Islam: The View From the Edge* (New York: Columbia University Press, 1998) and *Conversion to Islam in the Medieval Period: A Study in Quantitative History* (Cambridge, MA: Harvard University Press, 1980). While Bulliet focuses mainly on eastern Iran, Michael Morony's *Iraq After the Muslim Conquest* (Princeton: Princeton University Press, 1984) describes the situation to the west. H. A. R. Gibb, *The Arab Conquests in Central Asia* (London: Royal Asiatic Society, 1923) includes discussions of various religion-based resistance movements to Islamization in the eastern Iranian world.

Marshall Hodgson, Bernard Lewis, and others have written about the Iran-based medieval Isma'ili group known since Crusader times as the Assassins. Farhad Daftary debunks much of the prevailing misperception about the movement in his *The Assassin Legends* (New York: I. B. Tauris, 1994). Daftary has also authored a comprehensive study of Isma'ili Shi'ism, *The Isma'ilis: Their History and Doctrines* (Cambridge: Cambridge University Press, 1990), as well as a concise, though dense survey entitled *A Short History of the Isma'ilis* (Princeton, NJ: Markus Wiener, 1998). The esoteric Isma'ili cosmology is explored in Henri Corbin's *Cyclical Time and Isma'ili Gnosis* (London: Kegan Paul, 1983). Naser-e Khosrow's travelogue is available in English as *The Safar-nama of Nasir-i Khusrau*, trans. Wheeler M. Thackston, Jr. (Albany, NY: 1988).

Among the extensive works pertaining to Sufism the writings and translations of A. J. Arberry and R. A. Nicolson are still useful and in some respects unsurpassed. A more recent historical introduction to Sufism, with considerable attention to Iranian Sufis, is Annemarie Schimmel, *The Mystical Dimensions of Islam* (Chapel Hill, NC: University of North Carolina Press, 1975). Her *The Triumphal Sun* (London: Fine Books, 1978) is one of the most reliable and scholarly treatments of the great mystical poet Rumi. Other scholarly works on Rumi are Franklin Lewis, *Rumi: Past and Present, East and West* (Oxford: Oneworld, 2000) and William Chittick, *The Sufi Path of Love: The Spiritual Teachings of Rumi* (Albany: State University of New York Press, 1983). The illuminationist philosophy of Shehab al-din Sohravardi is the subject of Henri Corbin's *The Man of Light in Iranian Sufism* (Boulder, CO: Shambhala, 1978). Sohravardi's

*The Book of Radiance* is available in the English translation of Hossein Ziai (Costa Mesa, CA: Mazda Publishers, 1998), and his *Philosophical Allegories and Mystical Treatises* in that of W. M. Thackston (Costa Mesa, CA: Mazda Publishers, 1998). The later illuminationist philosopher, Molla Sadra, is discussed in Seyyed Hossein Nasr's *Sadr al-Din Shirazi and His Transcendent Theosophy* (Tehran: Imperial Iranian Academy of Philosophy, 1978).

Moojen Momen provides a detailed survey of Shi'ism in *An Introduction to Shi'i Islam* (New Haven, CT: Yale University Press, 1985). A good source on the roots of Safavid Shi'ism is Michel Mazzaoui, *The Origins of the Safawids: Shi'ism, Sufism, and the Ghulat* (Wiesbaden: F. Steiner, 1972). John Woods' *Aqquyunlu: Clan, Confederation, Empire* (Salt Lake City: University of Utah Press, 1999) outlines the dynamics of fifteenth-century Turkic tribal politics. Roy Mottahedeh's highly readable book, *The Mantle of the Prophet* (New York: Pantheon, 1985) weaves together five hundred years of Iranian Shi'ism as a backdrop leading up to the 1979 revolution.

The *ta'ziyeh*, or Shi'ite passion play, is discussed in depth in Peter J. Chelkowski, ed., *Ta'ziyeh: Ritual and Drama in Iran* (New York: New York University Press, 1979). Several humorous accounts of popular Shi'ite piety can be found in Terrence O'Donnell, *Garden of the Brave in War* (London: Ticknor & Fields, 1980). Books on the Persian garden include Donald Wilber, *Persian Gardens and Garden Pavilions*, second edition (Washington, DC: Dumbarton Oaks, 1979) and Mehdi Khansari, M. Reza Moghtader, and Minouch Yavari, *The Persian Garden: Echoes of Paradise* (Washington, DC: Mage, 1998).

CHAPTER 8: THE BABI MOVEMENT AND THE BAHA'I FAITH

To date most work on the Baha'i tradition has been by Baha'i scholars. The standard historical treatment is Peter Smith, *The Babi and Baha'i Religions: From Messianic Shi'ism to a World Religion* (Cambridge: Cambridge University Press, 1984). A detailed study of Babism can be found in Abbas Amanat, *Resurrection and Renewal: The Making of the Babi Movement in Iran, 1844–1850* (Ithaca, NY: Cornell University Press, 1989). The thought of Baha'u'llah is analyzed as a sort of precursor to post-modernism in Juan R. I. Cole, *Modernity and the Millennium: The Genesis of the Baha'i Faith in the Nineteenth-Century Middle East* (New York: Columbia University Press, 1998). Cole has also written numerous scholarly articles on various aspects of Baha'i history.

The articles and edited volumes of Moojan Momen and Denis MacEoin are also important for the academic study of the Baha'i faith. The late-nineteenth-century English Iranianist E. G. Browne had a particular interest in Babism and the Baha'i faith, and met numerous followers of these traditions during his travels in Iran, as recounted in *A Year Amongst the Persians* (London, 1893) and other works.

CHAPTER 9: RELIGIONS IN IRAN TODAY

There are many books written about Iran's 1979 Islamic revolution. Among the most balanced treatments of this highly contested historical event are Shaul Bakhash, *The Reign of the Ayatollahs* (New York: Basic Books, 1984), Said Amir Arjomand, *The Turban for the Crown: The Islamic Revolution in Iran* (New York: Oxford University Press, 1988), and Mohsen Milani, *The Making of Iran's Islamic Revolution* (Boulder, CO: Westview Press, 1988). Ruhollah Khomeini's essays on political theory are available in English as *Islam and Revolution*, translated and annotated by Hamid Algar (Berkeley, CA: Mizan Press, 1981), while those of Mohammad Khatami can be found in *Islam, Liberty and Development* (Binghamton, NY: Institute of Global Studies, 1998). The contemporary debates by Iranian religious scholars on issues pertaining to women are vividly evoked in Ziba Mir-Hosseini, *Islam and Gender* (Princeton, NJ: Princeton University Press, 1999). Several representative essays by Abdol Karim Soroush have appeared in English as *Reason, Freedom, and Democracy* (New York: Oxford University Press, 2001).

The vicissitudes of Iran's religious minority communities since the 1979 revolution are detailed in Eliz Sanasarian, *Religious Minorities in Iran* (Cambridge: Cambridge University Press, 2000). Sanasarian neglects to discuss the Mandaeans, who however are richly treated in Jorunn Buckley's *The Mandaeans*, cited above. Human rights organizations such as Amnesty International issue periodic reports on the treatment of religious minorities in Iran, as does the US Department of State. Many of these are accessible on-line.

# Index